DEATH AND THE CHRISTIAN

IS VOLUME

55

OF THE

Twentieth Century Encyclopedia of Catholicism

UNDER SECTION

V

THE LIFE OF FAITH

IT IS ALSO THE

61ST

VOLUME IN ORDER OF PUBLICATION

Edited by HENRI DANIEL-ROPS of the Académie Française

DEATH
AND THE CHRISTIAN

By JEAN-CHARLES DIDIER

Translated from the French by P. J. HEPBURNE-SCOTT

HAWTHORN BOOKS · PUBLISHERS · *New York*

First Edition, March, 1961

NIHIL OBSTAT

Hubertus Richards, S.T.L., L.S.S.

   Censor Deputatus

IMPRIMATUR

E. Morrogh Bernard

   Vicarius Generalis

Westmonasterii, die XXIV DECEMBRIS MCMLX

CONTENTS

PART I

MAN'S MISERY AND GOD'S SALVATION

CHAPTER I

MESSIANIC FORESHADOWINGS

Suffering and death are among man's deepest sources of anguish, as modern psychology makes so strikingly clear. Some try to avoid the thought of them, straining to gather rosebuds while they may, but none can escape them. The age-old complaint may be forcibly silenced for a while but is always ready to break out again: "No longer will your happy home give you welcome, no longer will your best of wives and your sweet children race to win the first kisses, and thrill your heart to its depths with sweetness.... Poor man, poor man! one fatal day has robbed you of all these prizes of life."[1]

The wisdom of the ancients was not always so earthbound, of course: it could face the inevitable with nobility. Socrates could say:

> Those of us who think that death is an evil are in error ... for one of two things—either death is a state of nothingness and utter unconsciousness, or, as men say, there is a change and migration of the soul from this world to another. Now if you suppose that there is no consciousness, but a sleep like the sleep of him who is undisturbed even by dreams, death will be an unspeakable gain.... But if death is the journey to another place, and there, as men say, all the dead abide, what good ... can be greater than this?[2]

[1] Lucretius, *De Rerum Natura*, III, 894–9. Trans. W. H. D. Rouse.

[2] Plato, *Apology*, 40. Trans. B. Jowett.

Marcus Aurelius was later to emphasize the inevitability of this law of nature and the worthlessness of this life:

> Despise not death, but cheerfully acquiesce in it as one of many acts ordained by the will of Nature. . . . Nothing will tend more to reconcile thee with death than to consider the objects thou wilt leave behind, and the morals of those with whom thy soul will no longer be involved. . . . What then is left to hold thee here? . . . Say, wilt thou not await in cheerfulness this end of thine, whether it be extinction or transformation?[3]

These two last quotations leave the door open to the hypothesis of survival. But only God knows how dark Hades is and how unsubstantial is the life of the shades, as far as we can judge from often conflicting assertions. And common sense easily outweighs philosophy: "Seek not to speak soothingly to me of death, glorious Odysseus. I should choose to serve as the hireling of another, of some portionless man whose livelihood was but small, rather than to be lord over all the dead who have perished."[4] For after all "it is sweet to see the light of day".[5]

It is in the mystery cults and the religions of salvation, to the extent at least that they did not grow decadent, that we find the hope of a blessed immortality in the light, that *lux perpetua* in striking contrast with the idea of a *somnus aeternalis*, analogous with annihilation.

No man can remain indifferent to this hope of immortality and survival. But how frail it is! At best, the soul is freed from the body, like the Greek "psyche" with butterfly wings, emerging from the chrysalis to fly to mysterious, embalmed retreats. And along with this hope

---

[3] *Meditations*, IX, 3 and V, 33. Trans. Jackson (Oxford, 1906).
[4] *Odyssey*, XI, 488–91. Trans. A. T. Murray (Loeb, 1946).
[5] Euripides, *Iphigenia at Aulis*, 1218–19.

in a life beyond death, what scepticism and doubt, what unashamed profession of materialism!

Even the Jewish religion seems only slowly and tardily to have accepted a serene concept of the future life. In Sheol there was room only for a ghostly life, without fulfilment or joy: "Brief, brief is my span of days; for a little leave me to myself, to find some comfort in my misery. Soon I must go to a land whence there is no returning, a land of darkness, death's shadow over it; a land of gloomy night, where death's shadow lies over all" (Job 10. 20–2).

It was the land of oblivion, where even the praise of God and hope in him were found no longer. "Thou hast no praise in the world beneath, death cannot honour thee; those who go down into the grave have no promise of thine to hope for" (Isaias 38. 18; cf. Psalm 6. 6; 117. 7).

On the same view of things the rewards of good and evil can only be temporal. We can understand how a reflecting soul like Ecclesiastes was tossed tragically to and fro between his faith in God and the twofold temptation, either to an epicurean enjoyment of life or to a universal pessimism: "all is vanity!"

And yet, after the Exile, Jewish religion was afforded certain glimmerings of fresh light. Here and there a voice was heard to sing of the hope of not going down into Sheol, of not remaining there but of living with God: "Thou wilt not leave my soul in the place of death, nor allow thy faithful servant to see corruption" (Psalm 16. 10; cf. 48. 16; 85, 13; 72. 23–4).

The book of Wisdom, of Alexandrian origin, magnificently expresses the idea of immortality in the presence of God (3. 1–7), while the idea of a resurrection of the body appears in Daniel (12. 2–3), Machabees (2 Mach. 7) and perhaps Isaias (26. 19).

But all these tendencies give the impression of being parallel rather than really convergent. In our Lord's time belief among the Jewish people was far from unanimous. The Sadducees did not believe in the resurrection of the body (cf. Matt. 22. 23–33; Acts 23. 6–10), and while the Pharisees, indeed, professed it, they seemed to conceive of it in a very down-to-earth fashion, unconnected with the vision of God. Full light was still to come.

Then one day, from his prison, John the Baptist sent messengers to the Man to whom he had formerly borne witness, asking him this question: "Is it thy coming that was foretold, or are we yet waiting for some other?" Perhaps John was finding it long to wait for the coming of the Kingdom and its judgement, which he had thought to glimpse (Matt. 3. 1–12). It was then that Jesus made him understand, by clear references to the prophet Isaias (26. 19; 29. 18f; 35. 5f; 61. 1), that the Messianic coming was accomplished. Now these references bore precisely on those works of power which accompanied the daily preaching of the Gospel: "The blind see, and the lame walk, the lepers are made clean, and the deaf hear, the dead are raised to life, and the poor have the gospel preached to them"; works of power, all of them, which repelled sickness and death and proved that the liberation of man's body was a sign of the Messianic age.

In fact, Christ's miracles are rich with an inexhaustible meaning: not merely manifestations of power in support of belief in a doctrine, but signs, pregnant with a whole divine mystery. No episode teaches this more clearly than that of the palsied man to whom Jesus said: "Son, take courage, thy sins are forgiven" (Matt. 9. 2). And when he heard murmurings, he replied: "Which command is more lightly given, to say to a man, Thy sins are forgiven, or to say, Rise up, and walk? And now, to convince you that the Son of man has authority to forgive sins while he is on earth (here he spoke to the palsied man), Rise up, take thy bed with thee, and go home."

Here we see Christ engaged in his primordial task, the forgiveness of sin and the struggle against evil. But the salvation he brings concerns the whole man; the Kingdom he inaugurates will not admit suffering and death any more than it will let the devil retain his hold: "Preach, . . . telling them, The kingdom of heaven is at hand. Heal the sick, raise the dead, cleanse the lepers, cast out devils" (Matt. 10. 7–8). That is why cures and raisings from the dead go hand in hand with the pardon of sins. The work of salvation is the liberation of the entire man, both body and soul.

What the Messianic work is to effect in us can be perceived through the medium of Christ's human nature. One day, indeed, during his mortal life, to three of his disciples he opened a window on the mystery of his person: "his face shining like the sun, and his garments becoming white as snow". This momentary transfiguration (Matt. 17. 2) revealed an order of things normal in itself, the reflection of the Word on the humanity he had assumed. Actually, what was abnormal was that this glory was usually veiled in him who represented in his person the Kingdom in all its power, but when, having suffered death, he rose from the grave, then his victory finally shone out through his humanity.

Behold him then, "firstborn from the dead" (Col. 1. 18) and our pattern; or rather, the one in union with whom we must be dissolved to have part in his death and resurrection and to live eternally in God.

But how? The Church has inherited the Messianic

function of the victorious strife against death, continuing Christ's work in the world. Nothing can be more instructive than to compare the mission given to the Twelve at the beginning of the public ministry ("Preach, . . . telling them, The kingdom of heaven is at hand. Heal the sick, raise the dead"—Matt. 10. 7–8) with the one given them after the Lord's resurrection ("You . . . must go out, making disciples of all nations and baptizing them"—Matt. 28. 19). The parallelism is obvious. And so the sacraments, like Christ's miracles, and in the same line with them, express, for the era of the Church, the presence of salvation, the action of the Spirit, the anticipation of the Kingdom.

As we know, baptism brings us into the mystery of Christ's death and resurrection (Rom. 6. 3–5), and the ancient catechetical instructions, such as that of Theodore of Mopsuestia, did not shrink from regarding us boldly as beyond death, as if it had been by-passed by the very reception of the sacrament. Moreover, theology does not hesitate to admit that baptism of its nature possesses sufficient efficacy to deliver us from all the ills of this life,[6] and this is true for the body as for the soul.

It is obvious, of course, that the man who has lived through our Lord's death and resurrection in mystery, and has thus acquired the right to return to Paradise and the paschal life, does not thereby enjoy, immediately, the complete and final liberation from evil which is nonetheless their logical consequence. The Christian remains at grips with sin, suffering and death. Theology can explain this, but for our purpose it is enough to say that the Spirit, whose action is the precise characteristic of the coming of the Messias (Acts 2. 14–21), has been given us as the "foretaste" (2 Cor. 1. 22; 5. 5) and the "first fruits"

[6] St Thomas Aquinas, *Summa Theologica*, III, 69, 3.

(Rom. 8. 23, Westminster Version) of the perfect liberation: "And if the Spirit of him who raised up Jesus from the dead dwells in you, he who raised up Jesus Christ from the dead will give life to your perishable bodies too, for the sake of his Spirit who dwells in you" (Rom. 8. 11).

And during this waiting, which marks out the period of faith and hope, all natural things are transfigured because of the new meaning they have received since Christ came.

Evil of course is a problem, one which unbelief transforms into an absurdity and a scandal. We all know the use made of the objection by the philosophy of the "Enlightenment" against belief in God.[7] The Christian, for his part, sees it as a trial; that is, first of all a danger to be fought against with the help of God, but also an opportunity of living more closely with Christ the mystery of the world's redemption (Col. 1. 24).

[7] See Paul Hazard, *The European Mind* (London, Hollis and Carter, and Newhaven, Conn., Yale Univ. Press), pp. 99 ff.

CHAPTER II

THE TRANSFIGURATION
OF THE CHRISTIAN'S
SICKNESS AND DEATH

The history of the Christian attitude to sickness has not yet been really studied. This is a pity, for we thus lack a very fine chapter in the story of Christian spirituality.[1] We can at least note some of its landmarks since Gospel days, when the grace of healing fought miraculously against sickness and infirmity in the name of the Messianic advent. The apostolic age and the succeeding generations were familiar with it, as St Irenaeus testifies.[2] This grace of healing did not disappear later: it would be unthinkable that God should withdraw from his Church, faced with the same problems of the coming Kingdom, the gift of which she disposed at the beginning of her mission.

Although healing has not disappeared we should look for it not so much in the realm of miracles—those of Lourdes, for example—as in that anointing of the sick of which we are about to treat, an organized charisma, a sacramental remedy.

[1] It has been broached by Abbé H. R. Philippeau in *La Maison-Dieu*, 15, pp. 53–81, "La maladie dans la tradition liturgique et pastorale". Evelyn Frost, *Christian Healing* (London and Oxford, 2nd ed., 1949), deals only with the Ante-Nicene Church.

[2] Quoted by Eusebius, *Ecclesiastical History*, Bk. V, c. 7 (ed. Lawlor and Oulton, London, 1928, I, p. 152).

What matters, behind this charisma or this sacrament, is the intention governing their use: the struggle against sickness on the strictly Christian plane, in an order of things directly connected with the eschatological Kingdom, where there will be no more "mourning, or cries of distress, no more sorrow" (Apoc. 21. 4). For sickness is an evil bound up with a sinful world, a world under the power of the devil.

But at the same time Christian thought on sickness is marked with the example of St Paul, who bears in his body the "stigmata", the scars of our Lord; his request for his cure is answered with "My grace is enough for thee" (2 Cor. 12. 9); he finally finds joy in his sufferings, in the thought that he helps to pay off in his mortal frame "the debt which the afflictions of Christ still leave to be paid, for the sake of his body, the Church" (Col. 1. 24). And on the other hand Christian piety fervently welcomes the words of Christ, who identifies himself with every sick person, saying: "I was sick, and you cared for me" (Matt. 25. 36).

It is around these two poles, the strife against sickness and the understanding of its mystical worth, that the Christian ages have revolved. Charity towards the sick, embodied in touching forms in the monastic Customaries,[3] and the respect for them shown by the Hospitallers' Orders, both prove, at the heart of the institutions devised for their benefit, the "eminent dignity" the sick were accorded. A whole liturgy was elaborated purposely to surround them with the Church's prayer and thus to assist them in their effort to be spiritually delivered and physically cured, or else to rise nobly above their pains.

As for the sick, they are made aware of their trial and,

[3] See the touching acts of attention to the sick prescribed at Cluny, in Philippeau, art. cit., pp. 76–8.

while asking for the grace to be released from it, they learn that it may be for them a means of purification, of sanctification, mystical identification with Christ crucified, and of praise of God. Certainly it is only the greatest souls who attain the heights: a Hermann Contract in the eleventh century, a Hermann Joseph in the twelfth, a St Gertrude in the thirteenth, a Margaret Ebner in the fourteenth, among others; not forgetting, in the East, the extraordinary figure of a Syncletica in the fourth century, who extolled her sickness as an expression of the glory of God.

But these examples, exceptional as they appear, are steeped in a whole atmosphere to which they belong, and on which they react in their turn. The medieval West gives clear testimony of devotion to Christ in his passion and frequent expression of the desire to suffer with him and imitate him is found. A whole spiritual literature, besides, developed and popularized the theme of "blessed suffering"; the treatise—*De duodecim utilitatibus tribulationum*[4] —had an incalculable influence on morality and spirituality. Ascetic writers thereafter felt the need to include some chapter on the good use of illness, and some of these are justly celebrated.

From the very outset, Christians were aware more easily how much death changed its aspect when seen through Christ, who had himself conquered death and saved the world by his own dying. The death of Christ appeared in very truth to his followers as the greatest act of love, the ideal passage from the world to God, the perfect sacrifice on behalf of all mankind, and his glorious resurrection projected its light through the gate he had opened.

[4] "On the twelve benefits of afflictions". This twelfth-century treatise seems to be the work of the Cistercian Gerald of Liège. Migne published it among the works of Peter of Blois: Migne, *Patrologia Latina*, 207, 989–1006 (hereafter referred to as *P.L.*).

For the baptized person, who has been mystically initiated into Christ's death and resurrection, even though he has yet to die, death can now seem only an imitation of his model and an accomplishing of the Paschal mystery.[5] Death has become a supreme act of faith and the crowning of that personal sacrifice which every Christian life offers to God, the definitive passing from sin to salvation "in Christ".

The Christian's death is, in literal truth, overwhelming in its grandeur and beauty. "God cannot behold any human death without being recalled to the presence of the death of Christ. A sight such as Calvary is not forgotten; the Father, if we may speak in an anthropomorphical manner which is here justifiable, never ceases to be moved by it. Seeing any man die, God sees again the death of Christ on the Cross."[6] On his side, man finds in this communion with Christ not only the certainty of eternal life and the resurrection of the flesh but the power to make the total gift of himself, in peace and joy, to the glory of the Father, for the crowning blessing of all is this: "Blessed are the dead who die in the Lord" (Apoc. 14. 13).

Much remains to be written about the attitude of successive Christian generations in the presence of death, starting with St Paul, for whom "death is a prize to be won" (Philipp. 1. 21), and the martyrs who went to their deaths as to a banquet. Certainly, on this point, there has been a noticeable evolution in Christian consciences in the course of the ages, from serenity to fear.[7] This is attested partly in a voluminous literature on the "Art of

[5] On this point, see L. Bouyer, *The Paschal Mystery* (Notre Dame, Ind., and London, 1950).

[6] R. Guelluy, "La mort du racheté", in the *Revue diocésaine de Tournai*, 1959, p. 89.

[7] See Philippeau, *art. cit.*, p. 60.

dying", as well as in art and even in the liturgy. No doubt it has sometimes had a warping or impoverishing effect. But the saints, and countless Christians following in their steps, have been able to give their deaths the full meaning they derived from Christ. St Teresa of Lisieux might well be afraid, in prospect, of not knowing how to die,[8] yet she died a beautiful death, saying, "My God, I love you!" And how touching is the reflection of the dying Suarez: "I never knew how lovely it was to die!" The deaths of monks, surrounded and sanctified by the ancient customs of the cloister, express an ideal put into practice. Every true Christian knows that "it is not primarily our life we must try to make happy and good, but our death", and that the greatest grace is not to be unaware of our dying but, on the contrary, to die in full consciousness, "peering through the door at our heart's desire".[9]

[8] *Novissima Verba* (Dublin, 1953), p. 137.
[9] G. Bernanos, quoted by Urs von Balthasar, *Le chrétien Bernanos* (Paris, 1956), pp. 418, 431.

CHAPTER III
THE CHURCH IN ACTION

The salient feature of the Christian attitude to sickness and death is a sort of assumption that the body, far from being forgotten, unconsidered or despised, is a constituent element of the human being, essential in its own right. This Jewish-Christian concept of the relation between soul and body is poles apart from a dualist philosophy, such as Platonism can be, and this contrast has its reaction in the strictly Christian teaching: the body is necessarily concerned with every idea of redemption and salvation offered to man. Bodily suffering and death affect the soul in its own being, and the eternal life of the soul can only find its perfect fulfilment by the resurrection of the body, just as even now in this life the health of the soul is closely bound up with that of the body. The Kingdom of God is offered not to "souls" but to "men and women", who consist of bodies as well as souls.

This was the purpose of Christ's miracles: to anticipate an integral salvation of man. And this is the rôle of the Church, to introduce us to the mystery of the same salvation, with the hope of its perfect revelation at the "last day". She fulfils this rôle through all her actions, from beginning to end of the Christian's life. Certain of her actions, being more specially endowed with supernatural meaning and efficacy, are called "sacraments" in the strict sense. Yet we must never forget that the Church is the great sacrament of salvation, and that her least actions

enfold us in an atmosphere of sacramentalism, in order
that the mystery of salvation may take possession of us.

That is why the Church multiplies her blessings: she
bestows them on all the day-to-day objects and the
humblest elements of our lives: on bread, oil, water, wine,
beer, eggs, butter, cheese, lard and new fruits, every food
and every medicine; she does this in order that we may
keep or recover our health of soul and body, that sin and
sickness may be driven off, that the power of Satan may be
broken and joy may possess us.[1]

The Blessed Sacrament itself is offered to us not merely
to produce grace and fervour in our souls but equally as
ordained for the health of the body. Cassian († 435) and
the Synod of Orange (441) order Communion to be given
to the "energumens" (possessed), to resist the attacks of
the devil and deliver the possessed from them.[2] St Caesarius
of Arles († 543) urges his flock to receive the Eucharist
as a remedy which preserves and cures on the two planes
of spirit and body.[3] The liturgy of the Mass itself affirms
the virtue of the Sacrament: *medicina sacramenti et
corporibus nostris prosit et mentibus; ad tutamentum
mentis et corporis; sit nobis reparatio mentis et corporis
caeleste mysterium.*[4] And in an even more explicit formula
it prays that the eucharistic sacrifice may purify us from
our sins: *quia tunc veram nobis tribuis et mentis et corporis
sanitatem.*[5]

[1] All these blessings are found in the Roman Ritual.

[2] Cassian, *Conferences*, VII, 30. Synod of Orange, can. 14.
(Hefele-Leclercq, II, pp. 442–3).

[3] Serm. XIII, 3; L, 1; LII, 5: CLXXXIV, 5 (ed. Dom Morin, I,
pp. 65, 216, 222, 710).

[4] "May the medicine of the sacrament benefit both our bodies
and our souls;" "for the protection of soul and body;" "may the
heavenly mystery be to us for healing of soul and body."

[5] "For then thou grantest us true health both of soul and of
body." Dom P. Bruylants, *Les oraisons du missel romain* (Louvain,
1952), I, No. 973, 994, 1065, 1099.

Very frequently the Church's prayer goes up for the benefit of our health, bodily as well as spiritual. Such prayers are found when she blesses the candles at Candlemas or the ashes at the beginning of Lent; and on Good Friday, in her "universal prayers", it is strictly physical healing that she requests for all the sick. In fact she does not even need any special occasion to frame her prayer thus: (*Concede nos*) "Grant to thy servants, we beseech thee, O Lord God, the grace to enjoy continual health of body and soul, . . . that we may be freed from our present sadness and rejoice in everlasting gladness."[6]

More especially when anyone is seriously ill, the Church surrounds her children with her prayer, her blessing, her encouragement, her spiritual help, her active charity. She has a whole liturgy for the visitation of the sick and puts at their disposal her greatest remedy, the *medicina ecclesiae*, the sacrament of Unction.

When death approaches she provides the Christian with his provision for the road, the sacrament of the great journey to the Lord, the Viaticum. Then she redoubles her prayers and solicitude for the one who is setting out for "the Father's house" and accompanies him to the very threshold of eternity, entrusting him then to the angels and saints, whom she summons to take over the charge from her; this is the "Commendation of the Soul".

After death, prayer still continues for the soul of the departed, while the body, through all the stages of the funeral liturgy till its committal to the earth, is surrounded with care and honour, in the name of the Christian faith in the resurrection of the body.

[6] Bruylants, *op. cit.*, 122.

PART II

THE SACRAMENT OF THE SICK AND THE RITES CONNECTED WITH IT

CHAPTER IV

THE SACRAMENT OF THE SICK: SCRIPTURE AND THE RITE

"Is one of you sick? Let him send for the presbyters[1] of the church, and let them pray over him, anointing him with oil in the Lord's name. Prayer offered in faith will restore the sick man, and the Lord will give him relief; if he is guilty of sins, they will be pardoned." So it is written in the Epistle of St James, 5. 14–15.

The Council of Trent, in its fourteenth session, committed itself to an authoritative definition of the meaning of this text:[2] it is a matter of faith that the Church here speaks of our sacrament of the Anointing of the Sick. The Apostle does not, of course, "institute" it but, in the Council's words, he "promulgates" and "commends" it to his readers. It follows naturally that its existence was already an established fact.

[1] Or "priests", in conformity with the teaching of the Council of Trent.

[2] We need not be surprised at the Church's deciding on the interpretation of a text of Scripture, thus exceeding in this field the limits accepted by scientific criticism, which rightly does not go further than its own possibilities allow. But the Church has the understanding of the Word of God because she possesses the Holy Spirit; she can see and read better than the scholars. This helps to explain Loisy's condemnation on this very point.

The institution of this sacrament, properly speaking, is something earlier. It derives, necessarily, from our Lord himself, and this too is a truth of faith which applies to all the sacraments, since Christ himself is their author. Some theologians have even thought they could find the origin of our sacrament of the sick in the text which says of the Twelve, sent on their mission by Christ, that "many who were sick they anointed with oil, and healed them" (Mark 6. 13). This text does, indeed, strongly suggest, on the one hand, the indubitable material continuity between the common ancient use of oil as a medicine,[3] and our sacramental anointings, and on the other, the undeniable parallelism, in the spiritual and religious order, between the charisma of healing in the Gospel period and our sacrament of the sick. Tradition, moreover, has not neglected this text: even before Bede († 735) who commented on it,[4] the Life of St Radegund[5] clearly alludes to it when it tells us that the saint used to anoint the sick with oil "in the manner of the Gospel". The Council of Trent, however, prudently declined to see in St Mark's phrase more than a preliminary statement, if as much: a mere hint or indication of the sacrament to come.[6] It is not easy, in fact, to discover the historical moment of the institution of each sacrament,[7] but of course that is not necessary for those who know how faithful the Church is in all her acts to the spirit and instructions of Christ: her tradition is one of unchangeable attachment and memory.

Furthermore, does not the question arise from posing

[3] E.g. in the parable of the Good Samaritan (Luke 10. 34).
[4] Migne, *P.L.* 92, 188.
[5] *More evangelico oleo superfuso* (*Monumenta Germaniae Historica*: scr. rer. mer., II, p. 370).
[6] The Council at first used the term *delineatum*, but finally preferred *insinuatum* in the final revision of its decree.
[7] Except for the Eucharist, of course.

the problem wrongly? Certain episodes in the Gospel may well, occasionally, give us a good view of the work of Christ, but in the aggregate they are only points of emergence in a progressive work which went on day by day: the founding of the Church was our Saviour's daily care, and the same is therefore true of the institution of the sacraments, which was coextensive and, as it were, identical with that founding.

However that may be, it is opportune to emphasize that "the sacraments were not born from the written texts".[8] The Church lived them, she performed and handed on their actions from the beginning, before the existence of any canonical literature, and *a fortiori* before any reference to it. This is precisely the case with the oil of the sick, and we may venture to say, in this instance, that it is fortunate. For while the Council of Trent laid down, as we saw, that the text of St James dealt with this sacrament, it must also be acknowledged that, for several centuries, not only did nobody interpret it in this sense, but, on the contrary, it was often positively understood in another way: by Origen, for instance, in his second homily on Leviticus.[9]

It was not till the beginning of the fifth century, in fact, with Innocent I and his correspondent Decentius of Gubbio, that we find a definite connection established between the text and the rite.[10] But the link connecting them is, from this moment, a definitely established fact. By itself, or handed on by Innocent and then by the Venerable Bede, the text passed from hand to hand down the ages, in

[8] Mgr Batiffol, in *Revue Biblique*, 1903, p. 528.

[9] Migne, *Patrologia Graeca*, 12, 417 (hereafter referred to as *P G*)

[10] The *Canons of Hippolytus*, can. 200, very probably allude to James 5. 14–15, but it is far from proved that they are earlier than the letter of Innocent I.

the service of the sacrament of the sick. Again it is worth noting that at first they argued more naturally from the rite to the text than vice versa: it was the rite which explained the text.

Little by little, however, the converse took place and James, more carefully studied, continually threw light on the rite and, as need arose, modelled it in several of its parts. So we have this form of anointing: "I give thee this anointing in the name of the Father and of the Son and of the Holy Ghost, that the prayer of faith may save thee and the Lord may raise thee up."[11] In a great number of ancient rituals the text of St James actually introduces the whole rite with this prayer, which the Roman liturgy has preserved, while displacing it to near the end:

> Lord God, who hast said through thy apostle James: "Is one sick among you? Let him send for the presbyters of the church, and let them pray over him, anointing him with oil in the Lord's name: prayer offered in faith will restore the sick man, and the Lord will give him relief; if he is guilty of sins, they will be pardoned:" cure, we beseech thee, our Redeemer, by the grace of the Holy Spirit, the ailments of this thy servant who is sick; heal his wounds and forgive his sins: drive out from him all pains of body and mind, and mercifully restore to him full health, inwardly and outwardly, that being recovered by the help of thy mercy, he may return to his former duties.

The sacramental theology elaborated in the twelfth and thirteenth centuries could not but continue in strict dependence on this text of Scripture and at the same time on the practice of the Churches, as we can judge from St Thomas Aquinas.[12] Finally and specially, the teaching of the Council of Trent appears as purely and simply a

[11] Theodulf of Orleans (Migne, *P.L.* 105, 220).
[12] *Summa Theologica*, Supplement, Qu. 29–33.

commentary on the words of St James. After quoting them at length, it declares: "By these words, as the Church has learned from the tradition of the apostles received from their hands, she teaches what is the matter, the form, the proper minister and the effect of this saving sacrament."[13] Further, the Council later affirmed that the words of St James constituted a "promulgation" of the sacrament, and that its use, as well as the rite used by the Roman Church, was in perfect conformity with the Apostle's text.[14]

The Council's exegesis was thus directed at replying to Protestant denials by expounding the Catholic doctrine on the anointing of the sick, starting from James 5. 14–15, and quite legitimately it read this text in the light of the Church's whole tradition, a tradition which is not confined to conceptual pronouncements but is above all a life. It is therefore only right that we should examine the practice of the Church and the behaviour of Christians through the ages.

[13] Session XIV, *On the institution of the sacrament of Extreme Unction.*
[14] *Ibid.* Canons 1–4.

CHAPTER V

HISTORY OF THE RITE: THE BLESSING OF THE OIL

We are the more bound to explore the practice of the Church and the faithful in regard to the oil of the sick, since, as we have said, this practice was established, down to the fifth century (Innocent I), without any reference to Scripture.

Now it must be admitted that the evidence for the use of the oil during this period is very rare: a text of doubtful import in St Irenaeus[1] in the second century; another, definitely probable this time, in St John Chrysostom about the end of the fourth.[2] The following piece of evidence, dating from the same period, is valuable to us because it shows us the practice of the laity: it concerns the wife of a Count Avitianus, who asked St Martin to bless, "as is the custom", a vessel of oil intended for a remedy in illnesses.[3]

"As is the custom": although we have no information, in fact, for the first four centuries on how the oil of the sick was used, the liturgical documents, on the contrary, give us prayers for the blessing of this oil which are very significant. We may set aside one found in a fragment

[1] Quoted by Eusebius, *Ecclesiastical History*, Bk V, c. 7, ed. Lawlor and Oulton, Vol. I (London, 1927–8), p. 152.
[2] *In Matthaeum.* Homily XXXII, 6 (Migne, *P.G.* 57, 384).
[3] Sulpicius Severus, *Dialogues*, III, 3 (Migne, *P.L.* 20, 213).

of the Coptic version of the *Didache*, discovered in 1924:[4] in spite of the esteem in which it is held by certain historians,[5] it is neither sufficiently authentic nor clear in its interpretation, nor of sufficient antiquity to compete with the formula of St Hippolytus in his *Apostolic Tradition*. This actually dates from the beginning of the third century and shows us a Roman practice. Its influence, moreover, was considerable in the East. We give it here in its simple and condensed sobriety: "O God, who sanctifiest this oil, as thou dost grant unto all who are anointed and receive of it the hallowing wherewith thou didst anoint kings, priests and prophets, so (grant that) it may give strength to all that taste of it and health to all that use it."[6]

Later on, the *Euchologion* or Prayer-book of Serapion of Thmuis († after 362), the *Apostolic Constitutions* (end of fourth century), and others too, show that in Egypt, Syria, etc., there was a blessing of oil for the sick. In the West the prayer from the *Apostolic Tradition* left a surprising mark on the formula of the Roman Pontifical, which is still in use and seems most probably to go back to the fourth century, judging by several signs and excepting several later amendments. We give it in the state in which it came to us from the eighth century:[7]

Send down from heaven, O Lord, we pray thee, the Holy Spirit, the Paraclete, on this richness of oil, which thou hast been pleased to draw from the living tree, for the refresh-

[4] Cf. J. Audet, *La Didaché, Instructions des apôtres* (Paris, 1958). pp. 67–70.

[5] Especially P. Boschmann, *Busse und Letzte Oelung* (Freiburg, 1951), p. 127.

[6] *The Treatise of St Hippolytus on the Apostolic Tradition*, 5, ed. G. Dix (London, 1937).

[7] Translated from *The Gelasian Sacramentary*, ed. H. A. Wilson (Oxford, 1894), p. 73.

ment of soul and body. And may thy holy blessing make of it, for all who anoint with it, drink it or touch it, a protection for the body (the soul and the spirit), banishing all pain, all sickness, all suffering of mind and body; this thy perfect Chrism, O Lord, with which thou hast anointed priests, kings, prophets and martyrs,[8] which thou hast blessed and which abides in our inmost being, in the Name of our Lord Jesus Christ.

These liturgical texts compensate for the regrettable scarcity of documents in the first Christian centuries, revealing an officially accepted authorized rite. Yet that is not their only advantage. They enrich our knowledge of the sacrament of the sick at this time by showing us that before the oil could be used it had to be blessed, in order to make it a sacrament and raise it to the strictly supernatural level. Everything that happens assumes, in short, that the sacrament of the sick took place in two stages: first the preparation of the holy oil, then its administration.

This explains both the action of the Christian woman, referred to earlier, who sent oil to St Martin for him to bless, and many other similar events in the course of time. In the fifth century, for example, we have St Geneviève, who often anointed the sick with oil; one day it happened that the jar of blessed oil she kept by her was found to be empty just when she wanted it for an urgent case. And she was all anxiety, says her biographer, "because there was no bishop within reach to bless it".[9] We

---

[8] The anointing of kings and priests recalls the Old Testament, as does that of prophets, though this latter example is somewhat doubtful. The anointing of martyrs is very difficult to explain, but in this connection there appears a curious resemblance between the Coptic liturgy and our own, on which may be consulted Dom E. Lanne, in *Irénikon*, 1958, pp. 138–55.

[9] *Vita beatae Genovefae* (*Mon. Germ. Hist.*, scr. rer. merov., III, p. 236).

draw attention to this point here, because it is typical of a well-established principle.

"Blessing" implies recourse to the Church, to the hierarchy whose intervention may be limited, as we shall see, to this blessing; but this intervention is preponderant in the subsequent use of the oil, and indeed indispensable to it, and from this derives the liturgical character it assumes, whatever variations in discipline may appear as between one Church and another.

In Rome, for example, the blessing is reserved to the bishop in the course of the Mass, in the place where we still find it today in the Mass of the Chrism; but before the seventh century it might be on any day, and "by request", we might say, for in those days it was the faithful who provided the oil and took it home once it was blessed, whereas nowadays Maundy Thursday is the only day in the year normally prescribed for it.

In Gaul, on the other hand, before the seventh or eighth century, the priest as well as the bishop is the minister of this blessing, which is given at any time and is not confined to the celebration of Mass; if the priest himself is to apply the blessed oil he blesses it just when he wants to use it. The same discipline is in force for Milan and goes on there till much later, apparently till the twelfth century. But finally, in one place after another, the Roman discipline prevailed.

THE ADMINISTRATION OF THE HOLY OIL

We have already noted that for several centuries the faithful, on their own initiative, used to bring to the priest the oil they wished to have blessed, and then to take it home as the "Church's medicine" against sickness. That the practice was general can be deduced from innumerable examples in the sixth and seventh centuries. The bishops encouraged it, moreover, partly, of course, to counteract the superstitions and magical practices so numerous and persistent in a population barely converted from paganism. St Caesarius of Arles († 543), for instance, and later St Eligius of Noyon († 660) earnestly commend this *medicina ecclesiae*: "Seek for health from Christ, the true light: have recourse to the Church, be anointed with blessed oil ..."[10] "When their children are ill, certain mothers run groaning and distraught and, what is worse, do not ask for the Church's remedy ... whereas they ought to anoint them, as it is written, with the oil blessed by the priests. ..."[11]

Caesarius did not preach to deaf ears and, in this particular case, it was the children who were bidden by their parents to be blessed with oil by the holy bishop.[12]

Surprising as it may seem to us at first sight, the fact is that the faithful themselves had the free disposal of this holy oil, just as they now have of the holy water. Priests and bishops, of course, after blessing the oil, did not fail to apply it themselves to the sick, as need arose. There is abundant evidence of this but we shall quote only one of the less explicit texts; we know from his biographer[13] that St Augustine used to hasten to go and see the sick who desired it, in order to lay his hands on them and pray at their bedsides. It is extremely likely that he was thus carrying out the counsel of St James, and that when he prayed he not only laid his hands on them but anointed them. This likelihood is increased by the author's very

[10] St Caesarius, *Sermons*, L, 1 (ed. Dom Morin, I, p. 216).
[11] *Id.*, LII, 5 (*ibid.*, p. 222).
[12] *Life of St Caesarius of Arles*, II, 17 (*Mon. Germ. Hist.*, scr. rer. merov., III, p. 490).
[13] Possidius, *Life of St Augustine*, 27 (Migne, *P.L.* 32, 56). (Ed. with English translation by H. T. Weiskotten, Princeton, N.J. 1919.)

clear allusion to a passage of St James' epistle a few lines before. Besides, none knew better than St Augustine himself the import of James 5. 14–15, for he incorporated it in his *Speculum* among the divine precepts which are binding on all Christians, and which he had gleaned from the whole of Scripture and collected in that book.[14]

Like Augustine, many holy bishops and abbots from the fifth to the seventh century were active in this ministry to the sick: Martin of Tours, Germanus of Auxerre, Caesarius of Arles, Germanus of Paris, Arnold of Metz, the abbots Sequanus and Eustasius, and others. Needless to say, the faithful preferred to resort to some holy person, both for the administration of the oil and for its blessing, and no doubt also, they relied more on his personal virtue as intercessor or miracle-worker than on the proper efficacy of the oil they used.

But this does not alter the fact that the laity had the free disposal of the oil of the sick, and that once it had been blessed by a priest or bishop—a strictly indispensable condition—they were allowed to use it themselves. The case of St Geneviève mentioned above is not exceptional, any more than that of the wife of Count Avitianus; both cases followed the normal practice during these times down to the Carolingian era, and throughout the Churches of the West. We repeat, it was normal and uncontested, and therefore canonically recognized and approved.

In that letter to Decentius already mentioned, Innocent I wrote as follows:[15]

> There can be no doubt that the text [i.e. of St James] must be interpreted of the faithful who are ill: it is they who can be anointed with the holy oil; once it has been made by the bishop, all Christians, and not only those who

[14] Migne, *P.L.* 34, 1036.
[15] Migne, *P.L.* 20, 559–61.

are endued with the priesthood, may use it to anoint themselves when they have need, they or their dependants. But
the rest [of the question] seems to us absurd, that is, the
doubt cast on the power of the bishop, seeing that the
priests possess it without any manner of doubt. There is
mention of "priests", in fact (in James 5.14) because the
bishops, hindered by other tasks, cannot visit all the sick.
If, however, the bishop has it in his power and judges it
opportune to go to see one, he can without hesitation pray
over him and anoint him with the holy oil,[16] being the one
to whom it pertains to make this holy oil.

This is quite categorical and admits of no interpretation,
such as some have later proposed, that would weaken the
force of the passage.

According to the Roman custom, the bishop has the
privilege of blessing the holy oil; all the baptized have the
right to use it themselves as their needs require.[17] The
liturgical data exactly correspond to this situation: during
these centuries we find a solidly constructed liturgy for
the consecration of the oil, but no ritual at all for its
administration to the sick: the faithful make use of it
according to very flexible rules.

[16] The text has *et benedicere et tangere chrismate*. As the very
next subject is the preparation of the holy oil in the course of
an argument *a fortiori*, the word *benedicere* cannot mean the
blessing of the oil. In connection with *tangere chrismate* it concerns the sick man, and only means the prayer and anointing
spoken of by St James. This prayer was certainly accompanied by
the laying on of hands and *benedicere* seems obviously to have
this precise sense, according to Galtier (*Dict. de Théol. cath* ... VII,
col. 1329).

[17] To say of St Geneviève that "the anointings she performed
had nothing sacramental about them, since she did not possess
the priesthood" (H. Lesêtre, *Sainte Geneviève*, Paris, 1907, p. 88),
is to project our own ideas into the past and to ignore a whole
body of incontestable facts.

Can we discover what use the faithful made of the oil of the sick during these same centuries? Several expressions which have survived later revisions in the consecratory prayers—we gave the text of two of them in an earlier chapter[18]—clearly prove that the holy oil could be taken as a drink. Several sources show that it was thus specially used for the dumb.

But it was in anointings that the holy oil was most often used: anointings which were ample and abundant, not at all resembling the timid and almost niggardly anointings of today; numerous and varied, even if not always an anointing of the entire body; sometimes repeated daily, like a regular medical treatment, for several days, with no limit to their duration and for as long as was required.

The parts of the body anointed vary according to the meaning attached to the anointings: when they are directly for cure, it will be the affected organ; when for relief in a wider sense it may be the head, the breast, the shoulders, etc.; when for a penitential purpose, it will be the organs of sense, the gates of sin.

In any case, there was no question of a merely physical medicine; but, as Innocent I said in the course of his letter, the oil of the sick, through the blessing it received, came into the category of "sacrament". It had therefore to be treated as such in whatever use might be made of it, and first of all, all profanation must be avoided. While the ordinary faithful had the free disposal of it, in that they performed the anointings on themselves, the unworthy, the public penitents officially deprived of the sacraments, were excluded from it. Further, although the use of the holy oil was not yet subject to the rules of a ritual, according to St James' instructions, it was accompanied

[18] Above, pp. 33, 34.

with prayer, prayer which was necessarily very simple and flexible in form, to be within the capacity of the laity.

The eighth century, however, marks a turning-point in the history of the rite. The use of oil as a drink rapidly disappears. For a time, longer or shorter in different Churches, the faithful still keep the right to perform the anointings (traces of it are found down to the twelfth century), but more and more a distinction is made between anointing by the laity and anointing by the priests. The latter steadily monopolize the administration of the oil of the sick, which is withdrawn from the hands of the laity. In future it will be for the Church to guard it, while imposing on the pastors the obligation to be more and more at the disposal of the sick.

It is now that rituals of anointing appear, and the administration of the holy oil takes on a strictly liturgical character. The wide improvisation which was the rule in former ages gives way to schemes which, while including many variants and fluctuations and even different trends of inspiration, yet represent an advance towards the crystallization of the rite.[19] The scheme adopted by Rome, and only finally imposed in the nineteenth century, is based essentially on the Cluniac customs of the early Middle Ages.

The rite is sometimes of astonishing length,[20] due as

[19] For a more detailed study of the history of the rite, see *Catholic Encyclopedia*, "Extreme Unction", by P. J. Toner.

[20] One of the most curious rituals in this way is that given us by Theodulf of Orleans († 821) in his *Capitulary* (Migne, *P.L.* 105, 220–2), which contains no less than fifteen anointings. There is no other ritual in the Latin Church with so many. But Theodulf draws from an important source, a Greek rite of his own period, and probably even older, the rite of a local church, which is confirmed by a manuscript from Sinai.

much to the prayers as to the actions (anointings, imposition of hands, signs of the cross) and the concelebration it involves, as well as to the psalmody during the anointings. The corporate character of the rite is also very marked; one ritual even concludes the administration of the sacrament with the kiss given by those present to their sick brother.[21] The anointings are often performed, as the text of St James suggests, by several priests, who divide the task variously in different rituals. In one, each of the officiants proceeds to his own anointing; in another, all recite, one after another, all the prayers; in another again, one priest reads the formula while another performs the anointings. Only the Eastern Churches have preserved to our days this custom of collegiate administration, that is, of the concelebration of the anointing of the sick, so that the rite is sometimes known among the Byzantines as the *heptapapadon*, because of the seven priests it involves. But in point of fact the Byzantine rite is here characterized not so much by its length as by its complication.

[21] Pontifical of Langres, thirteenth century.

CHAPTER VI

MODERN LITURGY AND DISCIPLINE

THE BLESSING OF THE OIL

As we saw from the consecratory prayer in the Roman Pontifical,[1] the oil which constitutes the matter of the sacrament is olive oil. Throughout the Mediterranean basin and from earliest antiquity, in fact, no other was known. It was in those days an absolutely primary and basic element of human life in many respects: food, light, personal toilet and sport, medicine. This last in particular was in constant use, in the form of drink or ointment, of which we have examples in Isaias 1. 6, Mark 6. 13 and Luke 10. 34. This is the oil referred to in the epistle of St James, the oil still required by the liturgy today. The expressed will of the Church makes its use a matter of validity.[2]

The blessing of the oil is another requisite for the validity of the sacrament.[3] In primitive times there was a

[1] Above, p. 30.

[2] *Codex Juris Canonici* (hereafter *CJC*), can. 937, 945. Does this mean that some other oil might one day be substituted for olive oil? It depends on the Church, for it does not appear to lie outside her power over the sacraments. In any case, it is certain that Churches in foreign lands, where the olive is unknown and cannot be acclimatized, would benefit by being allowed to use an indigenous oil.

[3] *CJC*, can. 734, 945.

general idea in vogue about the sacrament—that of the "vessel" which "contains" grace—according to which the sacrament consisted of the consecrated matter itself, independently of its use. Later theology, transcending this concept and placing the sacrament in the administration of the holy oil, held the blessing to be only the operation which makes the oil the "remote matter", fitting and indeed necessary for the sacramental action.[4]

In any case, from the very fact that the blessing of the oil is an essential condition for the existence of the sacrament, we should see it as something more than a bare preparation for it. It has sacramental value, and we shall not be wrong in regarding the sacrament of the sick as a sacrament which is effected at two points in time.

In the Latin Church this blessing of the oil of the sick is strictly reserved to the bishop. We know that it was not always so, at least in certain Churches. Even now, moreover, Canon Law provides that a priest, if duly authorized by the Holy See, can give this blessing.[5] As for the Eastern Churches, their traditions and rites, and consequently the priest's functions, are always safeguarded. The Council of Trent certainly had no idea of striking at the practice of these Churches, by which the priest blesses the oil when he needs it for the administration of the sacrament. On the contrary, Rome is most careful to maintain the Eastern customs with the utmost tact, and this one in particular.[6]

[4] The theologians are not so sure that the blessing necessarily requires the special formula appointed in the Pontifical. Many of the best, such as Capello, consider Extreme Unction to be valid when given with another consecrated oil, such as Chrism or the Oil of the Catechumens.

[5] *CJC*, can. 945; Council of Trent, Sess. XIV, can. 1.

[6] Thus the Congregation for the Eastern Church, by a decree of June 25th, 1933, granted to Coptic priests, without restriction, the power to bless the oil of the sick before anointing, "in conformity with the ancient use of the Church of Alexandria".

This blessing, we must remember, is reserved in the West to Maundy Thursday, no doubt by a process of attraction towards the blessing of the other holy oils. As early as the time of St Caesarius of Arles, advantage was taken of the moment when the holy bishop blessed the oil of catechumens to present to him also the oil to be blessed for the sick.[7] The same process must have been generalized and organized to give us the liturgical ceremony as we know it.

This ceremony, especially since the decree *Maxima Redemptionis* of November 16th, 1955 restored the Maundy Thursday "Chrismal" Mass, has preserved some of the majesty of the ancient rites. Twelve priests, seven deacons and seven subdeacons stand around the bishop. Once there was a genuine concelebration by the bishop and the priests, who together blessed the oil of the sick at the end of the Canon, as they had together consecrated the Eucharist. This "concelebrated" blessing of the oil of the sick still survived in some French dioceses down to the seventeenth century, but disappeared along with the concelebration of the Mass, or rather, it seems to have been assimilated to the blessing of the other holy oils. But even as now restricted to the vestiges of the ancient concelebration, the Chrismal Mass still remains one of the finest ceremonies of the liturgical year.

Every Mass of the Roman rite visibly preserves the point where, at the end of the Canon, the blessing of the oil of the sick used to be inserted, immediately before *Per quem haec omnia*; a relic of the primitive times when the oil could be blessed on any day of the year. It is still at this point that the blessing is made in our days, once a year, in the Chrismal Mass. Interrupting the Canon, the bishop pronounces a form of exorcism over the oil

[7] *Life of St Caesarius*, II, 17.

which has been presented to him, and then the magnificent epiclesis, *Emitte*. As we have already given its content[8] and noted its import, we need not insist on it further, except to point out the vigour of its expressions, invoking the descent of the Spirit, as if it were question of a divine presence in the material element, like the Blessed Sacrament. This of course is not so, but nonetheless we ought to recognize in the oil, because of its blessing, that divine virtue, effective for spiritual and bodily health, which we expect from it.[9]

Formerly, after the Mass, every Christian who had brought oil to be blessed took back his own and carried it home with him. But from the eighth century, as we have seen, things gradually changed and the faithful no longer had the right to keep it in their homes. In compensation, it became incumbent on the diocesan Church to distribute this oil to all the parish priests. This distribution sometimes assumed a solemn form. In our time, the distribution and forwarding of the holy oils from the cathedral to the different parishes has been planned and organized, in some places, with a view to a general realization of diocesan unity around the bishop, and to a better understanding of the sacraments, of which he is the source. To this is added a pilgrimage from the parishes to the cathedral; the symbolism of this pilgrimage is very rich and easy to understand.

[8] Above, p. 33.
[9] It is ordered by Canon Law (*CJC*, 734, sec. 2) that if the holy oil is running short a little unblessed oil can be added to it, even several times, provided that the added oil is less in quantity. We have here, then, a case of consecration by "contact". This is not a unique case: it is common practice for holy water, and used to be so too for the wine in the Mass: the Churches which have kept Communion from the chalice still practise it.

THE ANOINTING OF THE SICK

The sacrament of the sick depends, as we know, on the ministry of the priests, and when the Council of Trent defined that the "presbyters" mentioned by St James were those men, and those only, who had received the sacrament of Order in the Church from the bishop, it added that only the priest is the proper minister of Extreme Unction. The rôle of the priest, at first centred on the blessing of the oil, was later extended to the actual anointing, until it finally and totally excluded the laity from its administration: the teaching of Trent, then, simply confirmed tradition.

Canon Law[10] not only echoes the Council but adds supplementary instructions to make things more explicit and precise: the only valid minister of the sacrament of the sick is the duly ordained priest, but among all priests the pastor of the parish where the sick man lives,[11] being the "ordinary minister", possesses before all others the duty and the right to give this sacrament.

Because the anointing of the sick depends on the ministry of the priests, the *Ordo ad inungendum infirmum*, the manual for the liturgy of this sacrament, was incorporated into the rituals intended for the use of priests. Still it is found in certain ancient Pontificals:[12] the letter of Innocent I to Decentius in consequence figured in these

[10] *CJC*, can. 938.

[11] It is therefore to their parish priest that the faithful ought to turn, in the first place, for the anointing of the sick. It is true that necessity knows no law, and in that case no priest will refuse to administer the sacrament, permission being then rightly presumed. We may note that when the bishop is ill it is the cathedral chapter which has the duty of giving him Extreme Unction.

[12] As, for example, the manuscript Pontifical of Langres, quoted on p. 41, note 21.

pontificals for some time, as evidence of the right of the bishops to anoint the sick, even if they did not in fact make use of it.

We are now about to study this liturgy of anointing. But a preliminary observation is necessary. The rites of anointing appear to be combined with those of the Visitation of the Sick, Penance, Communion and finally preparation for death. Is this a merely material disposition of the pastoral rituals, setting out consecutively the various acts required to follow one another logically? Perhaps, but it would seem to be more: the compenetration of the various rites, their mutual transpositions, their overlapping in view of a consistent whole, suggest an intention of doctrinal import, even if this intention is earlier than any theological speculation on the sacrament.

All the same, this ritual collection, though apparently complicated, displays an eminently prayerful character, thoroughly in the spirit of St James. Again we must remember that our rite has been much cut down and appears somewhat curtailed when compared with many ancient rituals of anointing.

Coming into the sick person's room, the priest begins by wishing peace to all who dwell in the house and offers the crucifix to the sick person to kiss, then sprinkles holy water and, if necessary, hears his confession, and exhorts him briefly about the sacrament he is to receive.

There follow three prayers[13] which have no intrinsic connection with the rite of anointing, but they go very well with the sprinkling just made (one of them, *Exaudi,* concludes the present rite of the *Asperges* every Sunday),

[13] We might properly count only two prayers, *Introeat* and *Exaudi,* for the formula *Oremus et deprecemur* is simply an exhortation to prayer, addressed to those present, defining its sense and intention, and its normal place should rather be before than after the prayer *Introeat.*

and there is no doubt that they have been borrowed from the liturgy of the Visitation of the Sick: they are—especially *Introeat*—prayers of entry.

Next follows the general confession with the two prayers of absolution, *Misereatur* and *Indulgentiam*.[14] We are now on the threshold of the sacrament of anointing in the strict sense, and the priest speaks to the bystanders, bidding them pray during the administration of the holy oil to the sick person. The bystanders, in fact, have a part to play and a share to take in the performance of the rite: during the rite corporate and fraternal supplication is here raised to the level of a real liturgical and sacramental function, which is a point of great significance.

The rubric of the Ritual includes the seven penitential psalms with the Litanies of the Saints, though it authorizes other prayers. In this the modern Ritual is inspired by the ancient *ordines* which, at the risk of making the administration unduly long for an invalid (some rubrics are aware of this), inserted psalms and antiphons between the anointings, and included appropriate litanical invocations thoroughly adapted to the occasion.

After the preparatory prayers, the liturgy of Anointing really begins. First, a prayer of exorcism is said over the sick person:

> In the name of the Father and of the Son and of the Holy Ghost, may all the power of the devil be extinguished in thee, by the imposition of our hands and by the invocation of the glorious and holy Virgin Mary Mother of God, of her noble husband Joseph, of all the holy Angels, Archangels, Patriarchs, Prophets, Apostles, Martyrs, Confessors, Virgins, and of all the Saints. Amen.

[14] One cannot help thinking that either this *Confiteor* does double duty with the sacrament of penance already given, or that the latter would be better placed here than earlier, where it interrupts the prayers of entry.

This prayer appears for the first time at Laon, during the twelfth century. It may be remarked how naturally the invocations of the saints included in it suggest the Litanies prescribed during the anointings.

We should also take special note of the laying on of hands. This is not that one connected with Penance, as we find in certain *ordines*,[15] but that indicated by the Epistle of St James which St Caesarius performed and which later became general after the ninth century, until an *ordo* of Tours[16] obliged not only priests but layfolk to use it. As a matter of fact this imposition of hands disappeared from the Roman rite and was not reintroduced to the Ritual until 1925, though it kept a prominent place in the Milanese rite. This action gives expression to a prayer for blessing and here, above all, for healing.

After this, while the bystanders recite the psalms, the priest proceeds to the anointings. With his thumb dipped in the holy oil he makes a sign of the cross on those parts of the body prescribed by the Ritual. In case of grave necessity he might instead use a brush,[17] like the Eastern priests, for whom this is the common and regular practice.

In the past the anointings were many and various: thus Dom Martène's *Ordo* III prescribes them not only on the neck and the throat, between the shoulders and on the breast, the eyes, the ears, the mouth, the nose, the hands, the knees, the legs, the calves, the feet and the palms of the hands, but "on nearly all the limbs and on the place where the disease is most threatening".

The Roman Ritual is more discreet and requires the anointing only on the eyes, the ears, the nose, the mouth, the hands and the feet. Until not so long ago it used to add

[15] Dom Martène's *Ordo* II, for example.
[16] Dom Martène's *Ordo* III.
[17] *CJC*, can. 947, sec. 4.

the anointing of the loins, but this, which in the case of women had long been omitted out of a sense of modesty, was entirely suppressed by the Code of Canon Law[18] in 1917 and disappeared finally from the Ritual in 1925.[19] In addition, the same Canon provides that the anointing of the feet may be omitted for any reasonable cause.

It is evident that the Roman Ritual's choice of the parts to be anointed has fallen on the sense-organs, to which have been added the feet, the means of all our comings and goings, and the loins, regarded as the seat of the carnal passions (as, elsewhere, the breast, the epigastrum or the groin). Clearly the choice of these places has been dictated by the guiding idea that these sense-organs are the gates of sin, the remission of which is the appropriate remedy. The words repeated by the priest at each anointing simply underline the pardoning implications of the rite: "Through this holy anointing and his most tender mercy, may the Lord pardon thee whatever sins thou hast committed by sight" (hearing, etc.).

Are all these anointings necessary? No: they must be given, in normal circumstances, in order to be lawful, but no single one of them involves the validity of the sacrament. In case of necessity any one alone would be enough; it would be preferable, however, to give it on the forehead,[20] with the short formula provided for this case.

The anointing of the forehead raises a little problem

---

[18] Can. 947, sec. 2. From the same sense of modesty, the anointing of the breast, where it was ordered, was given at the base of the neck in the case of women (as in the Langres Ritual of 1679, for example: *in summa parte, juxta collum*).

[19] It is rather curious to observe that on August 14th, 1858, the Bishop of Utrecht, who had deleted the anointing of the loins from his Ritual in order to adapt the text to the custom, was ordered by the Congregation of Rites to restore it.

[20] *CJC*, can. 947, sec. 1.

which has left only one trace on the present Ritual. Formerly it used to be thought that a spot once consecrated by an anointing could not receive another. Therefore one who had been ordained priest could not be anointed again on the palms but only on the back of the hands. This custom is still in force.[21]

Having finished the anointings and cleansed his hands, the priest personally resumes the leading of the prayer, which the bystanders were supposed to continue during the anointing of the sick person. The triple *Kyrie Eleison*, followed by the *Paternoster* and several verses from the Psalms with their responses, so many glowing ejaculatory prayers repeated by priest and assistants in turn, are in fact the normal, traditional conclusion of the Litanies just recited. "O Lord, save thy servant: who hopeth in thee, O God" (Psalm 85. 2). "Be unto him, O Lord, a tower of strength: from the face of the enemy" (Psalm 60. 4). "Let not the enemy prevail against him: nor the son of iniquity approach to hurt him" (Psalm 88. 23).

The rite concludes with some collects. The Roman Ritual has three. The first—*Domine Deus, qui per apostolum*—the translation of which has been given earlier,[22] quotes the text from James in full: it is very ancient, certainly earlier than the ninth century; for most of the earlier period, it served as an introductory prayer to the rite of anointing, where it was much more suitably placed than it is now.

The next prayer—*Respice, quaesumus*—is of Ambrosian origin,[23] and is perfectly in place here. "Look down, O Lord, we beseech thee, upon thy servant N., exhausted with the infirmity of his body, and refresh the soul which

[21] Ritual, tit. 5, cap. 1, sec. 17.
[22] P. 30.
[23] Sacramentary of Bergamo.

thou hast created, that being amended by chastisements he may feel himself saved by thy remedy."

Finally, the prayer *Domine sancte Pater* is simply the collect from the Mass, in *The Gelasian Sacramentary*, of thanksgiving "for the restoration of health".[24]

O Holy Lord, Almighty Father, eternal God, who by pouring the grace of thy blessing upon sick bodies dost preserve, by thy manifold goodness, the work of thy hands, graciously draw near at the invocation of thy name, so that, delivering thy servant from sickness and bestowing health upon him, thou mayest raise him up with thy right hand, strengthen him by thy might, defend him by thy power and restore him to thy holy Church, with all desirable happiness.

The liturgy of Extreme Unction ends with these prayers.[25] By themselves, in spite of the complexity of the whole rite, they suffice to convey the meaning of the rite.

[24] *The Gelasian Sacramentary*, ed. Wilson, p. 282.

[25] It may be thought that in the present Roman Ritual the rite ends too abruptly. In France there used to be some splendid formulas from the Gallican blessings to conclude the administration of the sacrament. Here is an example from the Langres Ritual of 1679, but composed from much older elements: "God the Father bless thee. Amen. God the Son bless thee. Amen. May the Holy Spirit enlighten thee. Amen. May he guard thy body. Amen. May he sanctify thy soul. Amen. May he enkindle thy heart. Amen. May he guide thy reason. Amen. May he deliver thee from all evil. Amen. May he defend thee with his hand. Amen. And lead thee to the joys of heaven, for he liveth and reigneth, etc."

CHAPTER VII

THE EFFECT OF THE SACRAMENT

BODILY HEALTH

Since it is of faith that the anointing of the sick is one of the seven sacraments of the New Law instituted by Jesus Christ,[1] this rite bestows "a grace of the Holy Spirit"[2] for the salvation of the Christian who receives it, and this grace is specified by the rite of the oil, which represents and signifies it. All the ample, rich symbolism of oil with its properties and medicinal virtues (sweetness, penetration, refreshment and well-being, etc.) here come into play.

For the anointing of the sick is a remedy, and first of all a remedy with the object of bodily healing. To be convinced of this we have only to glance at the prayers from the Ritual we have already quoted.[3] This is also the sense of the text from St James: "Prayer offered in faith will restore the sick man, and the Lord will give him relief." Finally this is unambiguously asserted by the tradition of the Church down the ages, as we have seen, by the teaching of her doctors, the exhortation of her pastors to their people and the use made by the faithful of this *medicina*

[1] Council of Trent, Sess. XIV, can. 1.
[2] *Ibid.*, cap. 2 on Extreme Unction.
[3] Pp. 30 and 52.

Ecclesiae, a magnificent practical demonstration of Christian faith.

Accordingly the Council of Trent[4] did not hesitate to include this assertion in its doctrinal teaching on the sacrament of the sick, and the debates which preceded this throw a very clear light, in their discretion and moderation, on the text finally adopted. Even more categorical, if possible, is the instruction in the Ritual[5] which describes this sacrament as "a heavenly medicine, health-giving not only to the soul but also to the body".

The efficacy of the sacrament of anointing on the state of health of the sick when it is received in favourable conditions is confirmed by the experience of priests, so often called on to give it, the experience of doctors and nurses, the experience of the sick and their attendants. If there is not always an effective and total cure, there may be room for a provisional improvement in health or at least for a relaxation and easing in the psychical order, which will normally influence the physical.

> Such an affirmation, we know, will seem to sceptics somewhat naïve, or else, running another risk, will scandalize a type of abstract idealism, which refuses to compromise a sacred rite by contact with biological realities or to link the salvation of the spirit with the cure of the body. But Christ did not cure the sick with the sole end of creating symbols and showing himself to be the physician of the wounds of the soul. He was moved with real compassion at the sight of the ills of the flesh, and the Church, following his example, has pity on the person of the sick, on his body as on his soul, in order to restore him.[6]

The efficacy of the sacramental anointing on the body undoubtedly deserves to be studied closely on the experi-

[4] Sess. XIV, cap. 2 and can. 2 on Extreme Unction.
[5] Tit. 5. cap. 1.
[6] J. A. Robilliard, in *Initiation théologique*, IV, pp. 676–7.

mental plane. In any case it is certain that this effect on the body is not something in the miraculous order: the sacrament operates as a remedy. And that is why the priest ought to suggest it, and the faithful to request it, before it is too late: "The words of hope and the promises of cure which accompany the administration of Holy Unction are too often belied by the desperate condition of the sick"[7] and thus become an almost heart-breaking mockery. The sacrament ought to be given in such conditions that the intention of curing the illness may have a meaning, apart from any prospect of a miraculous intervention on God's part.

It is true that Tradition which we have been describing bears the mark of a change in the use and the concept of the sacrament of the sick.

There was a tendency to postpone the reception of Unction more and more, till the last moments, and to class it among the "Last Sacraments", even after the Viaticum. The arrangement of the different elements in the Ritual easily lent itself to this: there we find in succession the Eucharist, the Viaticum, Extreme Unction, the Visitation of the Sick, the Method of assisting the Dying, the Apostolic Blessing and Plenary Indulgence *in articulo mortis*, the Commendation of the Soul, the expiry and the obsequies. Again, the fact that in primitive times the holy oil was denied to public penitents increased the cases where it was postponed, with reconciliation, to the hour of death, and certain requirements or prohibitions, amounting to a sort of legal death, which sometimes resulted from reception of the sacrament, tended still more to put off its reception as late as possible, even to the last moments.

On the other hand, the concept of the sacrament elaborated by the theologians of the twelfth and thirteenth

[7] *Directoire pour la Pastorale des Sacraments*, sec. 58.

centuries, under the influence of certain principles and with a rigorous spirit of systematization, resulted in relegating the corporal effect of the Unction of the Sick into the background. Not all went as far as Duns Scotus, who did not even mention it, but many did not succeed in giving it its due place in their theory of the sacramental effect of Unction.

Obsessed by this idea that the effect of a sacrament can only be spiritual, and by the fact that bodily healing does not follow either necessarily or always, these theologians came to contrast the anointing of the sick with the gift of healing in the primitive Church; that is, they came to consider the anointing as essentially a remedy for sin, complementary to the sacrament of penance, with a view to a good death.[8] There were even some who saw Unction as a sort of seal and consecration to this end.

Finally, it had more than once been necessary, in the course of time, to combat heretical denials in order to defend the strictly sacramental virtue of the anointing of the sick. This was especially so at the time of the Protestant Reformation. It is not surprising that the Council of Trent presented the scholastic teaching, though with perfect mastery and consummate artistry of exact definition, to assert the efficacy of this sacrament. "If any one should say that the holy anointing of the sick does not confer grace, nor remit sins, nor relieve the sick, but has now ceased to exist, as if it had only formerly been a grace of healing [*quasi olim tantum fuerit gratia curationum*], let him be anathema."[9]

It is thus plain that while the Council denies the possi-

---

[8] The personal teaching of St Thomas Aquinas, which far transcends that of his contemporaries, will be found in the Supplement to the *Summa*, Qu. 29–33.

[9] Sess. XIV, can. 2 on Extreme Unction.

bility of Unction being *only* a charisma of bodily healing, it neither denies nor ignores this aspect. Its phrase "relieve the sick" (*alleviare*) is far too concrete not to envisage the body as well as the soul, and if further proof were needed we have only to recall that during its debates on this text the Council refused to add to this expression the adverb "spiritually", which would have excluded all physical effects.

Finally, theology legitimized, at least in appearance and in its own sphere, the postponement which had become increasingly common in the reception of the holy oil. Since the twelfth century, it had become the custom to describe the anointing of the sick as "Extreme Unction" and the "Sacrament of the Dying."[10] These expressions do not necessarily convey an exclusive position, but are nonetheless regrettable, at least from the pastoral point of view, in so far as they are likely to influence the mentality and practice of the faithful.

For this reason there is now a general tendency to substitute for these expressions others better founded in tradition and theologically more adequate, such as "the anointing of the sick" or the like. It is a safe example to follow, for it is given by the Magisterium of the Church.[11] Those who

[10] The Council of Trent itself, Sess. XIV, cap. 3, takes note of the fact that this last expression is current.

[11] We quote Cardinal Schuster, *Liber Sacramentorum*, I, p. 239, speaking of the "*Sacramentum Olei*, which only a fairly modern theology has called 'Extreme Unction', thus tending to give it that alarming meaning it has now . . ." Also Mgr Théas, Bishop of Tarbes and Lourdes, in his pastoral letter of 1953, *On the Sacrament of the Sick*: "'Extreme Unction' suggests that one receives it when one is in extremity . . . it would be desirable to call it instead the 'anointing of the sick' or the 'holy anointing'. . . ." Above all, perhaps, the *Directoire pour la pastorale des Sacraments* adopted by the plenary assembly of the bishops of France, sec. 58, and other recent papal documents, which certainly seem to avoid the word *extrema*.

are beset with pastoral problems can only be thankful for it,[12] for they know better than anyone else how important it is to extricate the anointing of the sick from the context of "Last Sacraments" in which it has gradually become embedded.

It remains, however, that while questions of words have their importance, the underlying reality is much more important. The teaching of Trent has been able to defend the bodily effect of the anointing of the sick, all the more remarkably when certain theological currents were against it. Even if theological thought has fallen out of step with the liturgy, as some have said, with regard to the holy oil, it is true that the liturgy remains unshakably orientated, by its prayers, towards the cure of the sick person. A renewal of attention to this privileged domain of theology is needed to recover the sacramental effect in all its dimensions. Theological research, moreover, will not have been in vain. It will have contributed to a true evaluation of the bodily effect of Unction in the totality of its sacramental action.

It draws attention, first, to the unity of man, made of body and soul, and to an equilibrium which rests on the health of the one as well as on the virtue of the other. The sickness of one becomes the sickness of the other, and every doctor knows that behind the sickness there is the sick man. Christ too knew this well, and that is why he attacked sickness at the same time as he attacked sin. The sacrament he instituted for the sick must be seen in this light: it is directed to the deliverance of the whole man, for the purpose of an integral salvation. Only a dualist conception of man, neither Christian nor Jewish, would

[12] From all these points of view the reader will have grasped why we only rarely use the words "Extreme Unction".

minimize the bodily effect of the sacrament by reducing it to a mere charisma of healing.

Again, by emphasizing the contingent and dependent character of the bodily cure, theology has not failed to compare this effect with the other effects of Unction and to deduce from it certain notes. The Council of Trent— following St Thomas, incidentally—considers it secondary and conditional, as a function of the spiritual effect and at its service.[13] The health of the body is considered in so far as it makes for the salvation of the soul.

Going further, the theologians have inquired how the sacrament produces its effect. They see it as often having a secondary effect, in consequence of the strictly spiritual effect, by a repercussion of the moral on the physical, and this may well be admitted, provided we are not content with a natural effect of a purely psychological order, but recognize it as an authentically sacramental, that is, supernatural effect. It is important, too, to emphasize the fact that the sacrament acts as a remedy, by a progressive improvement, not by a sudden change.

From this follows quite naturally a practical conclusion: the bodily effect of the holy oil must not be lost to view; the priest should administer this sacrament to the sick with the intention of curing them as well as sanctifying them, at least in so far as he gives it in conditions which allow of this. The sick person, for his part, should be prepared for it and welcome it in such a way that there may be no obstacle to its efficacy in this domain.[14]

THE FORGIVENESS OF SIN

St James says, of the sick person who receives anointing:

[13] Trent, Sess. XIV, cap. 2, on Extreme Unction. St Thomas, *Summa*, Suppl., Qu. 30, art. 2.

[14] St Thomas, *Summa*, Suppl., Qu. 30, art. 2.

"if he is guilty of sins, they will be pardoned." In marked contrast to the bodily effect, this spiritual effect of the sacrament of the sick has more and more dominated Christian thought and has gradually become the most conspicuous of the effects of the holy oil.

We know that sickness is linked to sin by an invisible bond, in this sense, first, that sickness is the consequence and fruit of sin. It was the first sin that introduced sickness into the world; but also in this other sense that sin is more formidable "for one who is also weakened by serious illness . . . and serious illness is more formidable for one who is weakened by sin": [15] sin, in fact, has disorganized the soul's command over the body, and the body which suffers from sickness weighs more heavily on the soul.

The Christian mind was more aware of this connection between sickness and sin when it lived by the faith and hope of the salvation brought by Christ, attested by every page of the Gospel, with his doctrine and his miracles, his redeeming death and resurrection. For a long time it even tended to identify, in this respect, sickness with diabolic possession, and to react in either case by recourse to the *medicina Ecclesiae*.

We can thus understand how St Caesarius and St Eligius promise both bodily healing and forgiveness of sins to those who receive the holy oil; how the liturgical texts couple healing and forgiveness together in their prayers for the sick; how sacramental penance with increasing frequency goes together with anointing, until the latter is practically considered to be the completion of the former and the fulfilment of an expiation which sickness makes impossible.

With the increasingly exclusive and deliberate choice of the sense-organs as the places to be anointed, and the

[15] Fr Mellet in *La Vie Spirituelle*, October 1947, p. 336.

meaning given to this choice by the accompanying formula
(. . . *indulgeat tibi Dominus quidquid deliquisti*), the sacrament of the sick was in practice dominated by this penitential aspect and the theologians, sublimating the notions
of sickness and medicine, came to define it as "a spiritual
remedy against sin", intended "to cure the disease of sin",[16]
at the risk of forgetting the effect of bodily healing, as we
have seen.

The Council of Trent had only to follow St Thomas
to consider the anointing of the sick to be "the consumma-
tion, not only of penance, but of the whole Christian life,
which ought to be a continual penance".[17] The fact that the
Council spoke of the anointing in the same session as the
sacrament of penance and immediately after it, is instructive enough in itself. Finally and most significantly, in the
second of the canons defining the Church's teaching on the
subject, the Council hurls its anathema against those who
deny the power of Unction to remit sins.

At the same time we must not forget another side of
the anointing of the sick. It is a "sacrament of the living"
and normally presupposes the state of grace. Tradition is
unanimous on this, from Innocent I, refusing the holy oil
to public penitents, down to our Rituals, which presume
the previous reception of Penance. Medicine is only given,
says St Thomas,[18] to the living, and is not the holy oil a
medicine?

How, then, are we to think of the spiritual effect of
Unction? To ascribe to it the forgiveness of venial sins is
correct, but this does not in any way define it more closely

[16] St Thomas, *Contra Gentiles*, IV, c. 73: *contra peccatum aliqua
spiritualis medicina*; *Summa*, Suppl., Qu. 30, art. 1: *institutum ad
sanandum infirmitatem peccati.*
[17] Sess. XIV, On Extreme Unction, preamble.
[18] *Summa*, Suppl., Qu. 30, art. 1.

than the other sacraments of the living, since normally this is the effect of every good work. We should therefore hold, with St Thomas, that this spiritual effect, being a sort of extension and completion of the work of the sacrament of penance, is a purification and more perfect cure of the soul, because it removes the after-effects of sin.

Even when they have been taken away, sins, both original and actual, leave a sort of scar on the soul which is always felt. The converted and pardoned sinner knows by experience that one can love God as generously after one's sin as before, but at the same time one feels weaker, less apt for the right, less resistant to the wrong, at grips with increased difficulties in the order of Christian life. These are the "after-effects" of sin for which the anointing of the sick is the remedy; not primarily the bad habits and dispositions springing from sinful acts, but this spiritual debility situated "in the zone of the facility, the aptitude and the inclination for the right."[19]

It is certainly permissible to suppose that, along with these after-effects of sin, the temporal punishment still due for sins is remitted to the sick person, at least in some degree, through the efficacy of a sacrament which is given him in order to make good for all his spiritual deficiencies.

As for the pardon of mortal sin, there are cases in which the anointing of the sick will take effect even there. This effect follows in special circumstances, indeed, but quite normally. This is proved by the practice of the Church, and by her interpretation of the text of St James. The anointing has this effect in the case of a sick person in a state of sin, who has not been able to have it pardoned through the sacrament of penance or an act of perfect contrition, and has since been deprived of his senses. In this case— provided that he has been freed from all attachment to sin

[19] J. A. Robilliard, in *Initiation théologique*, IV, p. 679.

at least by a sentiment of attrition—the sacrament of the holy oil will give him pardon of his sin and, in this precise case, will give it him much more certainly than sacramental absolution.[20]

Such is the magnificence of the mercy of God! But we must not trifle with it.

SPIRITUAL STRENGTHENING

Health of the body, pardon of sin; these two do not exhaust the sacramental effect of the anointing of the sick. That a cure does not always follow is a fact of experience and the Council of Trent does not hesitate to insist on its conditional character: (the sick man) "sometimes obtains health of body, when it is expedient for the salvation of his soul."[21]

The pardon of sin, too, is contingent, as the text of St James shows: "if he is guilty of sins, they will be pardoned." Therefore, if the efficacy of the sacrament is to be assured, it must be something more than these two conditional effects, and we must look beyond the conspicuous to the fundamental.[22]

To this search Christian thought has been devoted, gradually distinguishing the contours of the essential effect. What has emerged from this age-long effort of theology is a very rich and complex grace which, when necessary, incorporates in itself the two former effects. Yet it surpasses them, and can be defined as a spiritual strengthening in sickness. But what does this mean?

We were speaking, just now, of the "after-effects" of sin which are healed by the anointing of the sick (but

[20] Cf. Capello, *De extrema unctione* (Turin, 1942), p. 111.
[21] Sess. XIV, On Extreme Unction, cap. 2.
[22] These expressions are from Fr Mollet, *op. cit.*, p. 343.

must not be confused with the sin itself), and we have said that they represented a sort of weakness and heaviness in the soul which militated against the fervour and full growth of the Christian life. Their removal by the virtue of the sacrament is only one aspect, essential but negative, of this strengthening which defines the grace of Unction.

To understand this strengthening in all its dimensions and in its positive aspect, it is important first to grasp just how uncertain every sickness is in its issue, as it may lead either to recovery or death, and what a trial it is in itself, whatever its outcome. Under the weight of the physical trial, the mental and moral powers are in danger of being crushed: impatience, discouragement, disgust, despair, selfishness, confusion, bitterness, hardness..., how many temptations there are for an invalid! Add to these the attacks really made by the devil, and especially in the last moments, as the ancient prints of the "Art of Dying" tried to depict.

The grace of Unction corresponds to the uncertainty of sickness, with an ambivalence which provides the wherewithal either to procure recovery or to prepare for a holy death, because this grace looks to the sickness as such, with all its possibilities and eventualities. It is, therefore, neither solely a grace of healing nor solely a grace for a good death, but a grace for the time of sickness, before this has passed its turning-point, so to speak, for either issue.

The best proof of this—a proof of fact—is that the Church has never granted the sacrament of Unction to those who are facing death but are not ill, however certain and imminent the prospect of death may be. On this ground, it must be said emphatically that Unction cannot be simply defined as the sacrament of the completion of life. But further, to reserve this sacrament for the dying, as certain ages have done and as there is still too often a tendency to do, if it does not actually destroy its nature, confines its action to one direction. And if it is self-evident that it is supremely helpful to the dying (and "Extreme Unction must not be refused to a dying person who has left it to the last moment to ask for it or accept it"[23]), how much better it would be if they had received it earlier, when it would have had all its possibilities of effectiveness!

As for the nature of this grace, the Council of Trent describes it admirably when it speaks of this "grace of the Holy Spirit, whose anointing...relieves and assures [*alleviat et confirmat*] the soul of the sick person, stirring up in him a great trust in the mercy of God, by means of which he is supported and bears more easily the trials and travails of his sickness, and more easily resists the temptations of the devil, 'lying in ambush at his heels'."[24]

This passage says all: self-abandonment with full hope in the Lord, the relaxation and peace which possess the soul, the supernatural understanding of the trial and the strength which enables one to master it, the detachment and spiritual freedom which leave the devil no hold.[25]

Why should we be surprised, in these conditions, to see in some sick persons not only cures and amazing physical improvements but astounding spiritual transformations, with a serenity and greatness which compel admiration? The grace of the sacrament has been there, sanctifying the

[23] *Directoire pour la pastorale des sacraments*, sec. 58.

[24] Council of Trent, *loc. cit.*

[25] Some theologians have also tried to see in the anointing of the sick a sort of consecration. Is this due to consideration of the actual rite of anointing, or to the setting of death to which it has too often been postponed? They even spoke then of a "character" conferred by the sacrament. But these theories have not been retained by theology. The oil, here, acts as a medicine and not as a consecration.

sick man for life as for death. For, "none of us lives as his own master, and none of us dies as his own master. While we live, we live as the Lord's servants; when we die, we die as the Lord's servants; in life and in death, we belong to the Lord" (Rom. 14. 7–8).

CHAPTER VIII

THE SUBJECT OF THE SACRAMENT

Surprising as it may seem, there is no obligation to receive the anointing of the sick. The Council of Trent says simply that it is sinful to despise it.[1] Canon Law lays down that no one must neglect it and the most zealous care must be taken to see that the sick receive the benefit of it.[2] It is precisely from this point of view that we must see the question. Even though it is not ordered by any commandment of God or the Church, this sacrament has been instituted by Christ as a means of salvation. At the least, then, it is useful and may even be absolutely necessary; no one, therefore, can afford to make light of it.

The duty which thus lies on the sick person lies also, in consequence, on those attending him, who ought to be aware of their responsibilities and know how to discharge them, as an apostolic task. It follows that "even if it was wished to stop the priest, on the excuse that if the last sacraments were offered to the patient his condition might be dangerously aggravated, there should be no hesitation in suggesting them. One must trust in the 'grace of state' given to these sick people, which makes these rites much less alarming than they appear to those about them, who are in good health."[3]

[1] Sess. XIV, On Extreme Unction, cap. 3 and can. 4.
[2] Can. 944.
[3] *Directoire pour la pastorale des sacrements*, sec. 58.

To speak of duty when there is no obligation may seem paradoxical. But in fact this enables us to see that over and above written laws there is still, for the Christian, a logic of the Spirit which is binding on us, a sense of salvation which must be safeguarded, a loyalty to Christ which makes us go beyond the minimum.

The sacrament is provided for the faithful who are sick. We have already seen that the mere prospect of death, however certain and near, does not authorize its reception: the woman in childbirth, the soldier going into the attack, the condemned man awaiting execution, are not entitled to it. The custom of the Byzantine Church, by which Unction is given to all the faithful indiscriminately in Holy Week, can not be regarded as genuinely sacramental.[4]

Reading the ancient liturgical formulas, it is curious to see how widely sickness was interpreted in the early Middle Ages: liver attacks, dysentery, paralysis, lameness, blindness, dumbness; tertian, quartian and other fevers, dementia, headaches; pains in the limbs, the chest, the bowels, the marrow; abscesses, bites and sores, poisoning, mania; diabolic possession, enchantments and spells.[5] All these ills qualified the sufferer for the sacrament. One cannot help remarking that many of these are certainly not very serious. The assaults of the devil were also then treated like illnesses, both because of the connection readily assumed between sickness and the devil, and because it could be difficult to tell sickness from possession in all cases.

Things are quite different now: neither the possessed

[4] In the Uniate Churches Rome has retained the rite but, in order to avoid all confusion with the anointing of the sick, the formula is quite different.

[5] Cf. the Gallican-Visigothic formula *In tuo nomine* published by A. Chavasse, *Étude sur l'onction . . .*, pp. 64–8.

nor the infirm in the strict sense[6] (cripples, the deaf, dumb, blind, etc.) are admitted to anointing on this ground alone. Old age, on the other hand, is equated in this respect with grave illness.[7]

Another element, in fact, has to be considered: the danger of death. It is well known that in the Latin Church, from the Middle Ages, it became more and more the general and imperative tendency, not without some exaggeration, to restrict the anointing of the sick to those at the point of death. The Council of Trent would not go so far in its teaching, being content to say that anointing was to be given to the sick and particularly to those who were in proximate danger of death.[8]

The Code of Canon Law[9] requires that the sickness involve the danger of death, and when this danger is only doubtful the sacrament must be given conditionally—which is as much as to say that it considers the danger of death necessary for the validity of the rite.

It was not so, however, in the Latin Church in pre-Carolingian days. They were then much more inclined not to give Unction to the dying, precisely because they were about to die! In the few cases where we read of them doing so, it was still a cure which they persisted in seeking.[10] The Eastern Church, on the other hand, has never been concerned about the danger of death in granting the sacrament to the sick, and Rome has never imposed this point of western discipline on the Uniates.

Some have therefore wondered whether this clause, "danger of death", were not purely disciplinary and thus

[6] We must remind readers that the Latin *infirmus* means "sick" and not "infirm" in our sense.

[7] *CJC*, can. 940.

[8] Sess. XIV, On Extreme Unction, cap. 3.

[9] Can. 940 and 941.

[10] Cf. A. Chavasse, *op. cit.*, p. 193.

subject to possible modifications. However that may be, this clause, even taken literally, has not the restricted meaning which some have ascribed to it. It is perfectly legitimate to interpret it broadly: the danger of death, in fact, need not be immediate in order to exist, and every serious illness *ipso facto* involves this danger. Further, the degree of gravity in the illness cannot be estimated in itself and in the abstract, but only concretely and subjectively, in the sick person himself. Finally we must remember that in the anointing of the sick we have a sacramental remedy capable of procuring their recovery, and therefore to wait too long for signs of mortality in the illness before giving it must inevitably prejudice its curative effect, like a therapeutic treatment applied too late.

The spirit of the Church, moreover, favours this interpretation. A Roman decision of February 20th, 1801, clearly authorizes the administration of the sacrament, in missionary countries, to the sick for whom the prospect of death is only remote; and the recent *Directoire pour la pastorale des sacrements* for the use of the French clergy, "while reminding them that Extreme Unction may be administered only to the sick who are seriously ill", wishes them to correct "the common prejudice which turns the sacrament of the sick into the sacrament of the dying."

The present discipline of the Latin Church does not allow the benefit of sacramental Unction to children who have not yet acquired the use of reason, even if they are gravely ill, and in case of doubt it must be given only conditionally.[11] Without disputing the law, one may question its theological basis. While the spiritual effect of the sacrament can have no place in these children, the effect of physical cure is still possible and would suffice

[11] Can. 940 and 941.

to make its administration lawful in these cases. For several centuries, in fact, from St Caesarius to Theodulf, infants were by no means excluded from the sacrament of the sick. It is true that later the age-limit varied remarkably. But excellent theologians of our days do not hesitate to admit that there is no decisive, intrinsic reason in favour of the present discipline and, on the other hand, it is certain that a sick adult, baptized on his deathbed, can receive Unction immediately afterwards,[12] although in this case too the spiritual aspect of the anointing would be almost completely absent.

This sacrament is refused by the Church to those who continue obstinately impenitent and in manifest mortal sin, to those who have been excommunicated and refuse to submit to the conditions for their reconciliation, or have formally displayed their hostility to religion and its rites. It would not be respectful to their freedom as men to give them Extreme Unction after they had lost consciousness— unless, of course, they had previously shown their repentance in some way.

Apart from these cases the Church is extremely generous and authorizes the conditional administration of the sacrament to any sinner deprived of his senses, even if he has given no sign of repentance. She knows that in this man, unable to express his wishes, some spark of attrition may arise and that in this moment Unction is his last plank of salvation.[13]

Can one receive the sacrament of the sick several times? Answers to this question have varied according to different theological principles. We may ignore the answer based

[12] S. Congregation of Propaganda, September 26th, 1821.
[13] *Directoire pour la pastorale des sacrements*, sec. 61, 62. *CJC*, can. 942, 943.

on the idea of a character or consecration pertaining to Unction. The idea which has prevailed is that of a remedy. "And why should the remedy be forbidden," wrote Hugh of St Victor, "if the malady itself cannot be checked?"[14] St Thomas, however, makes less of the malady than of the danger of death.[15] From him we learn the right opinion, which remains inscribed in the discipline of the Church,[16] that the sacrament of the sick can be repeated when, after a cure, another grave illness follows or if, in the same illness, an improvement takes place, followed by a relapse. It is held that it is the same with prolonged old age or with an illness that extends over several years.

When we turn to the ancient practice of conferring Unction for several days following or by the ministry of several priests at once, we see that this was not a repetition, for then the sacrament preserved its unity under the whole series of rites. It is the same with all the concelebrations, and the idea throughout was that of a genuine "medical cure", by means of "the Church's medicine".

To conclude these pages on the sacrament of the sick, it is important to realize fully the richness of its benefits for those Christians who know how to welcome it. That is the heart of the problem, and its solution is to be found in a reform of men's mentalities which have been too often warped, if not superstitious, about Unction. The liturgical revival and the Christian community-sense which accompanies it are its essential factors. The mystery of the Christian life is perfected in this sacrament: every Christian must know how to open himself to it.

[14] *De Sacramentis,* II, 15 (Migne, *P.L.* 176, 578).
[15] *Summa,* Suppl., Qu. 33.
[16] *CJC,* can. 940.

CHAPTER IX

RITES CONNECTED WITH UNCTION: THE VISITATION OF THE SICK

Our seven sacraments are surrounded with a whole world of symbols, actions and objects—the sacramentals—which wrap the Christian life about in a very close network, making this life itself sacramental in its entirety. This is particularly true of the sacrament of the sick. The anointing is set in a vast context of prayers, rites and procedures, an ample liturgy surrounding the sick to sanctify them and take them up into the mystery of Christ.

We have already spoken of all the blessings poured out by the Church for the health of body and soul: a regular pharmacopoeia offered by the Rituals, containing blessings both of remedies in general and of materials for dressings and surgical apparatus. It will not surprise us to find there the blessing—in fact, several blessings—of an oil intended for the private use of the faithful, apparently as a substitute for the sacramental oil, but it is curious and significant that the form of exorcism used for this purpose is an old, obsolete form for the blessing of this sacramental oil.[1]

Not only does the Church bless the things provided for the sick person as remedies or otherwise; she blesses the

[1] Ritual, tit. 8, cap. 19. Cf. A. Chavasse, *op. cit.*, pp. 79–81.

sick person too in a special way, and we find several blessings of this sort in the Ritual: those of a sick adult, or pilgrim, or child,[2] not to mention that reserved to Benedictines, called the "Blessing of St Maurus". And these blessings comprise not only sprinkling with holy water but also laying on of hands—the charismatic gesture of healing—the recitation of prayers obviously borrowed from the Ritual of Anointing or the Visitation of the Sick.

In her prayers, the Church does not hesitate to associate with herself the intercession of the Blessed Virgin—*salus infirmorum*—and the whole host of saints, the "Auxiliaries" and the "Anargyri" (the moneyless), gladly ratifying popular devotion, with the sometimes curious specializations attributed by it to particular saints.

This is not all. It would be surprising if the Church's prayer did not culminate in the celebration of the Eucharist. Prayer for the sick is normally inserted among the intentions of every parochial Mass, a tradition preserved by the great intercessions of Good Friday as well as by the biddings from the pulpit every Sunday.

Our Missal also contains a votive Mass for the sick, taken from *The Gelasian Sacramentary*, in which the lessons are the Gospel story of the centurion at Capharnaum and the passage from St James on the anointing of the sick. It is used too seldom in our days, but it once held a prominent place in our sacramentaries and rituals of the sick.[3] In fact it was celebrated in the sickroom or in the church, and always in direct connection with the administration of the sacraments. We must remember too that the reception of Holy Communion then accompanied the reception of the holy oil, with the intention of the

[2] Appendix, 41–3, 48.
[3] E.g. in the Pontifical of Salzburg (*Ordo* XII of Dom Martène).

cure being prayed for, as we have noted above,[4] and St Caesarius, for example, used earnestly to urge his flock to use it.

Equally we must remember that it was during Mass that the oil of the sick was blessed, at least according to the Roman rite, and this became the discipline, so full of teaching, for the whole Western Church. Was it not fitting that this blessing should be joined to the eucharistic consecration, just as all sacramental efficacy is centred on the health-giving efficacy of the Body and Blood of Christ?[5]

Now, all this liturgy of the sick—sacraments and connected rites—is included in a wider framework, which the Roman Ritual calls "The Visitation and Care of the Sick."[6]

Acts of brotherly love, the visiting and care of the sick, are a duty for all Christians and bring their own reward: "Come, you that have received a blessing from my Father, ... I was sick, and you cared for me" (Matt. 25. 36). All the more, therefore, are they the duty of one who has the cure of souls. The instruction in the Ritual says: "It is not the least important part of his duties to have a care for the sick. As soon, therefore, as he hears that any one of his flock is ill, he must go to see him of his own accord, not waiting to be called; and not once only but as often as may be necessary. He will exhort his parishioners to inform him when anyone in the parish is ill, especially if the illness is serious."[7]

Besides the act of charity, the head of a community has the duty of knowing his sick parishioners at first hand, of forming an estimate of their quality as Christians; he

[4] Above, p. 22.
[5] Cf. L. Bouyer, *Liturgical Piety* (English edn *Life and Liturgy*), p. 175.
[6] Tit. 5, cap. 4.
[7] *Ibid*. Cf. *CJC*, can. 468.

should teach them again, if need be, the good news of the Kingdom and salvation, and revive their hope and courage; he should strive to raise them above themselves by union with Christ, and prepare them for the sacraments they will need.

That is why the old Sacramentaries so closely connect Penance, Unction, the Eucharist (as Viaticum or otherwise) and preparation for death with the actual Visitation of the Sick, often to the point of fusing them into one.

The pastoral duty of visiting the sick has in fact always been the priests' most keenly felt responsibility. With great zeal, psychology, tact, and apostolic spirit, they have made a great art of it (in the best sense of the word). Certainly the right approach to the sick is not something which can be improvised. The priestly tradition is full of noble examples of this art, and we have already had occasion to quote that of St Augustine.

But on the other hand it is important that the laity, both the sick and those who tend them, should know how to receive the priest, confidently, without deceit or fear, because they know what he is doing. He does not come merely to entertain the invalid, but neither does he come as the bearer of bad news. He comes to bring the sick man sanctification and healing, and therefore peace and joy, in the fullest possible measure.

It is moreover natural that in the heart of the Christian community the laity should fraternally take their share of the priest's responsibilities, in order to relieve him to some extent, if necessary (as is the case in large parishes). But the rôle of the laity is primarily to maintain and strengthen the communion in suffering and prayer of the parochial family with its suffering members.

Yet how many Catholics know that the Visitation of the Sick is a liturgical office in the Ritual? In arranging its theme the Church has been inspired by certain great aims: to pray for the sick person, to help him to pray himself, to let him hear a word of God's which will support him in his faith, his hope and his love. This liturgy has a striking flexibility: nothing is imposed, but all is left to choice, which is guided by circumstances and the sick person's own wishes, in fact, the whole can be abridged.

After the "Peace be with you" and the sprinkling with holy water, the priest will converse quite simply with the sick person, guiding the talk in a supernatural direction, to lead to an atmosphere of prayer. Then will be said a psalm, chosen from the first four Penitential psalms, or Psalm 90 (*Qui habitat*), followed by the versicles and responses and the three collects; finally, on leaving, the priest will give the invalid his blessing and sprinkle him with holy water.

The Ritual also offers four optional sequences, each consisting of a psalm, a reading from the Gospel and a prayer. The psalms (6, 15, 19 and 85) are specially appropriate for the state of the sick; the Gospel stories (the centurion at Capharnaum, the powers given to the apostles by the risen Christ, St Peter's mother-in-law and the cripple at the Sheep-gate pool) all inspire faith and trust, while the prayers ask for healing, being taken from the ancient rituals of Unction.

Then again we have Psalm 90, with a prayer, and that bold laying of hands on the sick man's head—bold in its expression of faith and obedience to our Lord's promise: "They will lay their hands upon the sick and they shall recover"—and finally that mysterious prologue to St John's Gospel which as early as the twelfth century we find incorporated in the Visitation of the Sick,[8] and then a final blessing.

[8] Missal of Remiremont (Dom Martène's *Ordo* XIV).

But again we must emphasize that the Ritual offers complete freedom in the prayers and meditations suggested to the sick person; some short prayers and ejaculations (verses from the psalms, the Our Father, the Hail Mary and the Creed), reflections on the Passion of Christ, the examples of the martyrs and the saints. All these prayers should be continued in the daily prayers of the family around and with the sick man.

Thus in prayer and love a whole Christian community is banded together round these sick members, and an atmosphere is created in which they can receive the sacraments and all those graces which may enable them to penetrate still further, in life and in death, into the mystery of the Lord's redemption.

PART III

THE SACRAMENT OF CHRISTIAN DEATH AND THE RITES CONNECTED WITH IT

CHAPTER X

THE VIATICUM

We have seen that Unction is the sacrament of the sick, not of the dying: in fact, healing is its normal, albeit conditional effect. Similarly, the Eucharist, by its sacramental nature, has a medicinal value which may extend even to the body,[1] as is intimated by the prayer of the Mass, "may it be to me a safeguard for body and soul, and a remedy."[2]

Furthermore, the real sacrament of completed lives, that which transfigures death and transposes it to the plane of the Christian mystery, is indeed also the Eucharist, inasmuch as it is the climax of Christian initiation.

We know the essential place of Easter in Christ's redemption, and how deeply his resurrection marks our supernatural life. It is his resurrection which guarantees us the complete fulfilment of the "good news", the coming of the Messianic kingdom and our personal salvation. Christ has associated us with his victory and has communicated to us his own life: through him we have overcome death to rise and ascend with him; we have become citizens of the heavenly city by the same right as the angels.

Yet we know that during this interval which divides the Lord's ascension from his return, all is still given us only

[1] Cf. above, p. 22.
[2] *Perceptio corporis tui*, before Communion. Cf. the last prayer in the rite of Communion of the sick.

as a foretaste. We are in the wilderness, between the Red
Sea and the Jordan, and our state is one of marching and
expecting, our time one of faith and hope. We are still
in the order of signs and figures, the sacramental order.

So the Eucharist is given us like the manna of the
Hebrews journeying to the Promised Land, like the bread
which fed Elias on the road to Horeb, the provisions for
the journey of the Christian till he emerges from darkness
into light. It is the supremely eschatological sacrament: it
is written into the pattern of the Kingdom of God, as an
anticipation of the heavenly banquet,[3] "until he [Christ]
comes" (1 Cor. 11. 26). It is participation in the "bread of
angels", that is, communion in the Word, in faith; it is
the sign of the new and completed covenant (1 Cor. 11. 25);
it is the source of eternal life in us: "The man who eats
my flesh and drinks my blood enjoys eternal life"
(John 6. 55).

The Eucharist of the early Christians was always gazing
forward to the last times and the Lord's parousia. "Gather
together thy holy Church from the four winds into thy
kingdom ... May Grace come and this world pass away!
. . . Maran atha!"[4] Moreover the theology of the great
Schoolmen is still faithful to that fervour:

> This Sacrament prefigures the possession of God which
> we shall have in our heavenly country, and under this aspect
> it is called *viaticum*, for it provides us with the means of
> coming thither; and again for this reason it is called
> *Eucharist*, that is, "good grace", for as St Paul says
> (Rom. 6.23), "the grace of God is eternal life"; or else
> because it contains Christ, who is full of grace. In Greek
> it is also called *metalepsis*, or "assumption", because, as

[3] Cf. Matt. 26. 29; Mark 14. 25; Luke 22. 29–30.
[4] *Didache*, 10. 5–6 ("Ancient Christian Writers", ed. J. Kleist, VI,
p. 21).

St John of Damascus says, "through it we assume the divinity of the Son."[5]

The Eucharist is thus clearly revealed as the sacrament of supreme hope and joy.

The eternal life here offered us is not just any sort of immortality. Not only the soul but the body has part in it, in the sense that the body will be raised up on the pattern of the body of Christ on the first Easter morning. For, says St Paul, "if the Spirit of him who raised up Jesus from the dead dwells in you, he who raised up Jesus Christ from the dead will give life to your perishable bodies too, for the sake of his Spirit who dwells in you" (Rom. 8. 11). Now this glorious resurrection of our bodies will itself be the fruit of the Eucharist, for our Lord has determined the direct relationship between them in his sermon on the Bread of Life: "The man who eats my flesh and drinks my blood, . . . I will raise him up at the last day" (John 6. 55).

> Knit to Christ as members to our Head, how can we end in the dust of earth, while the Head is reigning in glory? What manner of Body would that be which, with its Head crowned in heaven, would have its feet for ever buried in the grave? Let us recall, too, that grace ushered in by the Eucharist, and transformed in heaven into glory, qualifies the souls to communicate themselves with all their glory to the flesh. With a desire that is overpowering, because inborn, these blessed souls long for their bodies as their natural complement; while to animate them again without at the same time glorifying them is no longer possible . . . On the last day, wheresoever the Body of Christ shall be in the person of his inanimate members, there shall

[3] St Thomas Aquinas, *Summa*, III, Qu. 73, art. 4. The Mass of Corpus Christi has magnificently preserved this teaching, as also the antiphon *O sacrum convivium*.

the eagles—the holy souls of paradise—also be gathered together from the four winds, to raise up that which had been struck down, and to build up in all its parts the finished and glorious Body of the Son of God, whose glory once more shall have swallowed up completely the very last traces of corruptibility and mortality (Matt. 24. 28; Luke 17. 37).[6]

These last lines touch on the "how" of the action of the Blessed Sacrament on the body. The explanation is to be found in a sane view of the unity of our being and the relations between soul and body. Through sanctifying grace, penetrating and modifying the soul, not only in its faculties but to its inmost depths, that is, to its substantial being as "form" of the body, the latter is now called the "temple of the Holy Ghost". One day, similarly, it will be made alive again, from the dust it was, under the restored influence of the beatified soul. For so long as the soul is separated from the body, it longs after the body for the sake of that complete happiness for which our nature is destined. This happiness the soul cannot have without the body. All this is the work of the sacrament.

From the earliest days, we find many witnesses of the Christian faith magnificently emphasizing the power of the Eucharist to bring about the resurrection of the flesh. "Our bodies," writes St Irenaeus, "through the Eucharist which they receive, are freed from corruption and possess the hope of rising to eternity." To Gelasius of Cyzicus, the Body and Blood of Christ are "the sacraments of our resurrection", and Leo XIII asserts that the risen body of our Lord deposits in our bodies "a seed of immortality".[7]

Hence the necessity of the Eucharist for salvation. Christ

[6] M. de la Taille, S.J., *The Mystery of Faith and Human Opinion* (London, 1930), p. 28.

[7] These passages and many others will be found in M. de la Taille, S.J., *Mysterium Fidei* (Paris, 1921), pp. 492–6.

had stated it himself in his sermon on the Bread of Life
(John 6. 54): "Believe me when I tell you this; you can
have no life in yourselves, unless you eat the flesh of the
Son of Man, and drink his blood." The Church, for her
part, ratifies this while clearly defining its meaning. Communion is not necessary for children under the age of
reason,[8] although some of the Fathers, and those by no
means obscure, have held such necessity to be so certain
that they made it their point of departure to prove the
necessity of infant baptism.[9] But from the age of reason
it is of obligation for all, at least once a year, and that at
Easter. The choice of that date is rich with instruction for
our subject.

If every Eucharist, then, is a sacrament of immortality—
and at every Communion we make the priest says: "The
Body of our Lord Jesus Christ preserve thy soul unto
everlasting life"—it is at the hour of the Christian's death
that the Eucharist is most certainly necessary, as the
sacrament of faith and hope in this everlasting life, in
defiance of all the powers of death, henceforth vanquished
by Christ.

The Eucharist is necessary in the hour of our death for
another reason, that it is the sacrament of charity, that is,
of our union with the Church, outside which there can no
more be salvation than outside Christ himself, for it is his
mystical Body. For this very reason the early Church
hastily reconciled penitents at the point of death, even if
their official penance was not completed, in the conviction
that the Lord, finding them in communion with the
Church, would give them his own peace.

[8] Council of Trent, Sess. XXI, cap. 4 and can. 4.
[9] For instance, Innocent I, *Letter to the bishops of the Council
of Mileve* (Migne, *P.L.* 33, 785); Gelasius, *Letter* VII (*P.L.* 59,
37–8); St Augustine, *Letter* CLXXXVI, 28–9 (*P.L.* 33, 826).

Finally, this necessity of the Eucharist in the hour of death derives from the fact that it expresses and actualizes our whole life in its sacrificial aspect, in and through Christ's own sacrifice. What is sacrifice, really, for a man, but the passing over, throughout his life, from sin to God, by a profoundly interior movement which hands him over bodily to be made perfect in the joy which God offers him, the joy of union with himself? And is not death, for this reason, the crown of life, the great passing from the world to God, our private "Easter", and so the supreme sacrifice to offer, in total self-oblation and for eternal joy in God? But this is only possible in Christ and by the Eucharist, which is the sacrament of his sacrifice, and which exists to take our sacrifice up into his and to give their meaning to our death and our life.

For all these reasons man needs his "journey-provision" when he is at grips with death. The Eucharist is his "viaticum", and that is why the Church makes its reception at this moment a very special and grave obligation.[10]

A special obligation, not in the sense that one's last Communion is theologically of different sacramental value from any other, but because it meets the supreme demands of this unique moment and, for this reason, underlines more strongly than ever the churchly, sacrificial and eschatological nature of the Eucharist. A special obligation, because the Church, by her whole attitude in this situation, understands this precise commandment to proceed directly from the words of Christ in John 6. 54, and therefore to be of divine law. So it is laid down that even if one has already received Communion that day, one should communicate again the same day, if the danger of death arises in the meanwhile.

[10] *CJC*, can. 864. Several of the following details are quoted from canons 853–69.

And the obligation is very grave. We saw that the anointing of the sick does not bind, strictly speaking, as a commandment. The Viaticum, on the contrary, in the eyes of the Church, is a peremptory precept, in virtue of which all measures of positive law are envisaged, and before which, when the case requires, even the strictest of them must give way.

It was for the Viaticum that reservation of the Blessed Sacrament was instituted, so that the Eucharist might always be accessible to the dying. So reservation is precisely the privilege, and the duty, of all churches and chapels whose incumbent has the cure of souls (the local ordinary, the parish priest, the superior of a community, etc.), because its sole end is not merely eucharistic devotion but the administration, whenever required, of the Viaticum.

If it is necessary to give Communion to a dying person, and the reserved Eucharist is not available, the priest must celebrate Mass expressly for this purpose, whatever the day or hour, even though he has said a previous Mass, or is not fasting, or even though it is an aliturgical day, like Good Friday, or Holy Saturday.

In case of need, any priest, even suspended or excommunicate, is empowered to administer Viaticum.[11] If the priest is not present or if, in certain kinds of illness, the administration of the sacrament requires special skill, then the laity, both men and women, are entitled to take his place, a fact which more and more needs stating, when so many parishes are without priests. If necessary, it can be given under the species of wine, or according to another rite than that of the dying person. It can even be obtained from an Orthodox church. The dying person can even communicate himself.

[11] *Ibid.*, can. 2261, sec. 3.

It used to be common practice, but is no longer allowed,
to give Viaticum to the dying who are breathing their last
or have lost consciousness; on the contrary, it is recom-
mended to give it to them without delay, while they are still
fully lucid.[12] It should be noted, incidentally, that one who
is about to die is not necessarily ill and may even be in
good health: the soldier going into the attack, for example,
or anyone going into serious risk of death through certain
tasks (pyrotechnists, test pilots, etc.) or in certain circumstances, such as bombing in war, religious persecution, etc.

Finally, even in times of local interdict, exception is
always made for the dying, especially as to the Viaticum.[13]

Thus through all these prescriptions of ecclesiastical law
the command of the divine law is plainly seen. The earliest
evidence of a law of the Church in this matter is found in
canon 17 of the Council of Nicaea in 325. This again only
recalls an "ancient rule". "The ancient and regular rule is
to be continued; that if anyone is at the point of death he
is not to be deprived of the last and most necessary viaticum." And it is well known that the Church's first care
has always been to ensure that the faithful should have the
sacrament of her communion, even if up till then they had
been denied it. It was one of the chief concerns of St Cyprian of Carthage after the persecution of Decius.

At the same period, St Dionysius of Alexandria recounts
the following curious incident, concerning an old lapsed
Christian called Serapion. About to die, he implored that
his sins might be forgiven and he might be restored to the
Church. His grandson

> ran for the presbyter. But it was night and he was unwell
> and could not come. Yet since I (Dionysius) had given an
> order that those who were departing this life, if they be-

[12] This last remark applies to mental patients.
[13] *CJC*, 2270, sec. 1.

sought it, especially if they had made supplication before, should be absolved, that they might depart in hope, he gave the little boy a small portion of the Eucharist, bidding him soak it and let it fall in drops into the old man's mouth. Back came the boy with it and when he was near, before he entered, Serapion revived again and said: "Hast thou come, my child? The presbyter could not come, but do thou quickly what he bade thee and let me depart." The boy soaked it and at the same time poured it into his mouth, and when he had swallowed a little he straightway gave up the ghost.[14]

Such, then, was the universal custom, and nothing is more moving than this desire of the early Christians, as shown in so many instances, to die taking their "journey-provision" with them, even in their mouths, according to the ancient Roman custom. In our days, we must admit, this appetite for the Viaticum seems very jaded in many Catholics. Ought they not to be reminded of the faith, the hope and the joy which it brings, but of which they seem all too ignorant?

There is another aspect of Communion as Viaticum which ought to be made clearer. The solemnity of this Last Communion is emphasized; now this solemnity derives largely from its aspect as an act of the Church. For our part we cannot admit a sort of dislocation, as some have viewed it, between eucharistic Communion and the communion of the Church, a sort of no-man's-land between the Church and the hereafter which, with the Viaticum, is the domain of purely divine law. As we have said, every Eucharist is an act of the Church, and the Viaticum can only be so in the fullest sense. Even to penitents excluded from all participation in the sacraments, even to condemned men handed over by the Inquisition to the

[14] Related by Eusebius, *Ecclesiastical History*, Bk VI, c. 44 (ed. Lawlor and Oulton, pp. 213–14).

secular arm, it has always been the Church's intention, in giving them the Eucharist in the hour of death (for it is to her alone that it belongs and it is from her alone that we receive it), to reconcile them, to bring them back into her unity so that God may find them there when they meet him; *in ecclesium interim suscipi et in ipsa Domino reservari*, in the words of St Cyprian.[15] The Eucharist is the sacrament of communion both with God and with the Church, and by its means the Church leads the Christian to the end of his pilgrimage and hands him over to the Lord.

It is therefore important to have a clear idea of the ecclesiastical aspects of the Viaticum. The rites accompanying it are nowadays reduced to their simplest form; the only difference from the usual form of Communion is in the words pronounced by the priest when placing the Body of Christ in the mouth: "Receive, brother (*or*, sister), the Viaticum of our Lord Jesus Christ, that he may preserve thee from the malignant enemy and bring thee to everlasting life."[16] But after all, does not the prayer accompanying all our Communions express the same eschatological outlook in almost identical terms? Or rather, our daily Communions have borrowed this prayer, with its eschatological bearing, from the ancient rituals of the Viaticum.

In times past a much fuller liturgy included very splendid rites, eloquent with symbolism. There was the recital of the Our Father and the Creed, the dying person's solemn profession of faith in the presence of the Church, and that sublime kiss of peace given by the dying man to all

[15] *Letter* LV, 29 ("to be received meanwhile into the Church and in her to be kept for the Lord").

[16] Some ancient Rituals (e.g. Dom Martène's *Ordo* XXIII) added also: "and may he raise thee up at the last day, when he shall come to judge the living and the dead."

his brethren whom he was leaving behind. Mass was celebrated to consecrate the Viaticum, sometimes the dying
man was present together with the community. Even now,
at least according to law, we have the presence of the
community, called together to accompany the Viaticum
in procession into the dying person's room,[17] and it is the
privilege of the parish priest, as head of the parochial
community, to take it to him.[18]

But who would not be astonished to discover, under
the rite of Communion for the dying, the exact reflection
or continuation of the rite of Christian initiation? As the
community is directly concerned in the entry of each of its
members into its company, so it is concerned in his
departure, and it is actively present at it, at least in the
person of its head.

The recital of the Our Father and the Creed corresponds
to their "tradition" before baptism in the presence of all,
and if, in practice, the required profession of faith is often
confined to an act of faith in the Blessed Sacrament, that
is only the result of an evolution which at some point has
forgotten its starting-point.

The solemnity of the "Last Communion" resembles that
of the "First Communion". The viewpoint of war against
the devil, mentioned in the formula of Viaticum, is precisely
that of the whole of Christian initiation, while that which
concerns everlasting life is its most authentic crown.

Finally, the farewell kiss corresponds to the kiss, so well
known to the first Christian centuries,[19] given to the neophyte, by which his older brothers welcomed him into

---

[17] Ritual, Tit. 5, cap. 4, sec. 10 ff.

[18] *CJC*, can. 850. To give Viaticum to the bishop, the cathedral
chapter is the authorized body (can. 397).

[19] St Hippolytus, *Apostolic Tradition*: St Cyprian, *Letter* LXIV;
Testament of our Lord Jesus Christ; Canons of Hippolytus,
139–40.

their communion. Several rituals have attached this kiss to Unction rather than to the Viaticum, and some liturgists have tried to interpret it in various ways; its significance is in fact connected with the rites of initiation.

In reality, the moving grandeur of Viaticum comes from the fact that it is the sacrament of Christian death. It transfigures it by taking it up into the Mystery of Christ and giving it the meaning of an initiation to everlasting life and the glory of heaven. "I shall not die, but live, and shall declare the works of the Lord" (Psalm 118. 17).

CHAPTER XI

RITES CONNECTED WITH VIATICUM: THE COMMENDATION OF A DEPARTING SOUL

People often speak of the loneliness of the dying. But the dying Catholic is never lonely. The Church, far from abandoning him after Viaticum, stays by his bed, inspiring his prayer and praying with him and for him to the last moment.

Nowadays it is chiefly in religious houses that this attendance of the community of the brethren is an actuality. We can all feel the spirit of brotherhood displayed by this rubric in an ancient Ritual of St Ouen of Rouen, quoted by Dom Martène:[1] "When they hear the signal [for the agony] all the brethren run up; and though among us it is forbidden to run, in this case all run, as if there were a fire: indeed it is an order ... The whole community must run to the spot, for they must always be present at the hour of death."

But this brotherly presence round a deathbed ought not to be the monopoly of the monasteries: religious, as such, are simply Christians who carry the logic of their baptism to perfection, and conversely every Christian in

[1] *Ordo* XIII.

the Church forms part of an assembly of brothers. So we can recall with emotion how, one summer afternoon, we saw the entire population of a village in the Black Forest, gathered in the church and praying, while the priest was somewhere in the village, by the bed of a dying man.

Even when the priest is alone, the whole Church is mystically present in him beside the dying. But perhaps we no longer realize how earnestly the Church urges that the priest should be called, when the time comes for a Christian to die. The priest, for his part, despite his many tasks, must at least be faithful to it, as to one of his primary duties, and one laid on him, moreover, by the Ritual and Canon Law.[2]

The first reason is not merely that he may bring some psychological comfort to the dying person or his household. It is something very different. The death of a Christian must be seen, in its deepest reality, as a liturgical celebration and a mystery of faith. And it is the work of the sacrament—the Viaticum—to hallow it by making it, unlike the deaths of the heathen, a "death in Christ".

But, as we have said, the sacraments are not to be thought of as isolated acts, cut off from everything else, more or less curtailed, moreover, and reduced to the strict minimum required for validity. We must respect the broad context of the acts and prayers of the Church—the liturgy —of which they are an integral and indeed primary part, with a meaning and import common to both. Prayer and sacrament, so far from being independent of each other or, what is worse, contrasted, are indissolubly bound together in the heart of the liturgy.

So the Ritual offers us a whole collection of secondary rites, designed to sanctify and consecrate the Christian's death, in a line absolutely identical with that of the Viati-

[2] Ritual, tit. 5, cap. 2, No. 15. Cf. *CJC*, can. 468, sec. 2.

cum. This was the more evident formerly, since the Viaticum was in practice given at the hour of death and therefore in the immediate context of those prayers, in the framework of "what is to be done for the sick who are in their agony", as the titles of the ancient Rituals express it.

There is no doubt that this collection of prayers is rather complex and even fairly composite. Divided into so many distinct chapters, we find a "Manner of assisting the Dying", a form of "Apostolic Blessing and Plenary Indulgence in the hour of death", the rite of "Commendation of the Soul", and finally some invocations and prayers for the actual moment of expiry,[3] without counting the prayers after death.

Further, all the Christian ages, including our own, have stamped the commendation of a departed soul with their own spirituality, in some form of prayer (some prayers to Christ in his Passion, for instance; an invocation to our Lady; a mention of St Joseph or other saints) and above all, perhaps, by certain more fundamental tendencies which appear, for example, in its penitential elements.

The apparent complexity of this collection is also certainly the result of the varying pastoral preoccupations which have been added in the course of the ages, largely through a sort of compenetration of several sacramental rites (Penance, Unction and Eucharist) in a group of "Last Sacraments", with the consequent theological implications. And if we may regret one thing, it is that the post-Tridentine Ritual, in its legitimate concern for reform and abridgement, has eliminated or displaced some precious elements of the authentic "liturgy of Christian death", while the collection still retains, nevertheless, its composite character.

But we may thank God that the rubrical directions of

[3] Ritual, tit. 5, cap. 5–8.

the Ritual are here intentionally flexible, allowing us to take into account our actual situations (conditions of persons and of time) and thereby to overcome the complexity of the amalgam by a judicious choice, when necessary, between its various parts. It is obvious, of course, that circumstances seldom permit us to exhaust all the possibilities of the rite of the dying. "Following it step by step, prayer shapes and adapts itself to the rhythm, now slow, now rapid, of the vanishing life."[4]

It remains true that from all the actions and words of this ritual a unity emerges, complex though we called it at first, and this unity is something very real, for it lies in the Church's intention to do everything possible to make the death of her children humanly and Christianly great and noble as a victory.

If we bear this last remark in mind we shall be in a better position to pick out the principal features which give our liturgy of departure its distinctive character. Our aim is not so much to follow the existing order of rites or to trace its history as to discover its internal logic.

In the first place we notice the Church's care to suggest to the dying person thoughts and sentiments worthy of a Christian, indeed necessary for his salvation: faith, hope, charity, contrition, forgiveness for injuries, acceptance of sufferings and filial abandonment to divine Providence. Now, as has often been observed, some chosen passages from the Gospel can stimulate devotion even better than abstract consideration or stereotyped "acts". It is only natural, therefore, that readings should be provided from our Lord's sublime priestly prayer (John 17) and from the Passion according to St John.

The better to help the dying man to pray, the priest

[4] H. R. Philippeau, in *Archiv für Liturgiewissenschaft*, 1955, p. 63.

also offers him the crucifix to kiss. Two prayers, unfortunately separated from the rite to which they normally belong, define the meaning of this kiss; there is first the invocation of the Cross: "We adore thee, O Christ, and we bless thee, because by thy holy Cross thou hast redeemed the world";[5] then a prayer in the true spirit of medieval piety, recalling in detail all the painful stages of the Passion: "O God . . . by thy holy Cross and thy death, deliver me from the pains of hell and vouchsafe to bring me where thou didst bring the thief crucified with thee . . ." The crucifix holds an important place in the ritual of the agony.[6] It must remain before the eyes of the dying person to the end, to inspire in him "the hope of his salvation".

The Ritual then gives a certain number of brief invocations to be said to the dying person, so that he may repeat them, at least mentally. Several of them will be murmured afresh at his last breath, particularly the name of Jesus. We know how devotion to the holy name of Jesus developed in the West between the twelfth and fourteenth centuries, and in this connection we may well recall Joan of Arc, dying with the cross she had asked for before her eyes, and on her lips the thrice-repeated cry of "Jesus!" Truly, all the piety of past centuries is reflected in our Ritual.

But these ejaculatory prayers, excellent as they may be in practice, have not nearly the traditional character and inspirational value of the psalms. These already formed part of the Jewish liturgy, and our Lord died with Psalm 21 on his lips. It is not surprising that the psalms were ordered to be recited, or rather sung, around the dying man so

[5] Cf. *Ordo* of St Eligius of Noyon (VIII of Dom Martène), where the invocation is in the singular.

[6] This importance has been rather a disadvantage, since it has proved detrimental to sacramentalism in the true sense.

that he might associate himself with them. The lives of the saints are full of examples of those who died while repeating the psalms, and men loved to remember the last words they then pronounced. For St Nicholas, for example, it was Psalm 30. 6 ("Lord, into thy hands I commend my spirit"); for St Peter Nolasco and St Louis of France, Psalm 137. 1–2 ("I will praise thee ... I will sing praise to thee in the sight of the angels, I will worship towards thy holy temple and I will give glory to thy name".); for St Francis of Assisi, Psalm 141. 8 ("Bring my soul out of prison, that I may praise thy name: the just wait for me, until thou reward me.")

Thus, not only does the Church inspire the prayer of the dying and rouse him to prayer, but she truly prays with him to the point of taking his place and making his prayer her own.

Finally she prays for him, and it is here that her rôle becomes almost essential. Without emphasizing it, we should notice all the penitential element which has penetrated this prayer for the dying, from the early Middle Ages onwards, in proportion as a graver anxiety about salvation weighed more heavily on every death, and the humility of the saints willingly joined hands with the penitence of sinners. This explains the presence of the prayer *Deus misericors, Deus clemens*, organ and witness of the Church's "reconciliation", which comes down to us from *The Gelasian Sacramentary;*[7]

> O merciful God, O God most kind ... grant [to thy servant N.] a full discharge from his sins ... Renew in him ... whatsoever has been vitiated by human frailty, or by the frauds and deceits of the devil, and bind him fast, as a member of redemption, to the unity of the body of

[7] *The Gelasian Sacramentary*, ed. H. A. Wilson, p. 66. (From the reconciliation of public penitents at death.)

the Church. Have compassion, O Lord, on his sighs, have
compassion on his tears, and admit him, who has no hope
but in thy mercy, to the sacred gift of thy reconciliation.

Other penitential forms occur elsewhere too: the first
phrase of the prayer *Delicta juventutis*, which comes from
Psalm 24. 7; the end of the prayer *Commendo te*, which
has been handed down to us from St Peter Damian
(† 1072); the three "devout and profitable prayers" of
medieval origin which are found at the end of the ritual
of the dying and, of course, the plenary indulgence attached
to the Apostolic Blessing, a general absolution granted for
the moment of death, and introduced into the ritual of
departure only in the eighteenth century. And need we
remind our readers of the ancient penitential rite, now
obsolete except in certain monastic orders, according to
which the Christian was laid to die on a bed of ashes or
straw?

Ought we to see a penitential aspect in the litanies included in the ritual of the dying? If we connected them
with the text of the litanies found in the ancient rituals and
the strict dependence they there have on the penitential
psalm, we should really do so. At the same time, these
litanies *ad mortem* have a tonality all their own; though
short, in the present Roman rite, they invoke not only
those saints who are most representative of spiritual aid to
the dying (St Joseph, St Camillus, St John of God, etc.),
but those who were our spiritual ancestors from the beginning of the world and form one Church with us—Abel,
Abraham and all the patriarchs, the prophets, the just of
the Old Testament; all the petitions, moreover, are for the
dying person: "pray for him—deliver him". These petit-
tions, which transcend the strictly penitential aspect, can
very well be incorporated in the last group of prayers, of
which it remains to speak.

Among the whole collection of prayers for the dying, this is, strictly speaking, the "Commendation of the Soul", designed for the last moments. Here we find the most moving elements of the liturgy of Christian faith, those most charged with meaning and the most traditional, where the Church's prayer takes a new turn. Now it is the official discharge accorded to the dying:

> Go forth, Christian soul, out of this world, in the name of God the Father Almighty, who created thee; in the name of Jesus Christ, the Son of the Living God, who suffered for thee; in the name of the Holy Ghost, who was poured forth upon thee ... may thy place be this day in peace and thine abode in holy Sion. (Psalm 75. 3).

The Church on earth has led her child to the frontier of her domain, which is this present life; on the threshold of the life beyond, her task accomplished to the utmost, she entrusts him to the Church of heaven. And to this end—convocation rather than invocation, it has been called —she calls on the angels and the saints:

> Come to his aid, all ye saints of God; run to meet him, angels of the Lord, receiving his soul, offering it in the sight of the Most High.—May Christ receive thee, who hath called thee, and may the angels lead thee to Abraham's bosom:
> May the angels lead thee into paradise: at thy coming may the martyrs receive thee, and lead thee into the holy city of Jerusalem. May the choir of angels receive thee, and with Lazarus, who once was poor, mayest thou have eternal rest.

In the present Roman rite, these two passages have their place after death. But it was not always so, and in certain rituals "the dying person might himself sing his own *Subvenite*"[8] (or at least hear it, may we say). In any case,

[8] Dom Gougaud, in *Ephemerides Liturgicae*, 1935, p. 18.

the uncertain position of these texts only reflected the
uncertainty about the precise moment of death and the
desire to express the full meaning of this supreme act in a
liturgy which is continuous from the agony to the burial.

But all the other prayers equally, in more or less the
same way, evoke the heavenly court. The Church begs all
the angels and all the elect to come to meet the dying
man, to rejoice over him and ensure him a place among
them:

> Mayest thou be placed among the companies of the
> blessed, and enjoy the sweetness of the contemplation of
> thy God for ever . . .

> Let St Michael, the archangel of God, whom thou hast
> appointed chief of the heavenly host, receive him: let the
> holy angels of God come forth to meet him, and lead
> him to the holy city Jerusalem: let blessed Peter the apostle,
> to whom God gave the keys of the kingdom of heaven,
> welcome him . . .

In the Gospel itself we read of Lazarus, the poor man,
carried by the angels into Abraham's bosom (Luke 16. 22),
and we find the rôle of the *psychopompi*, the "soul-con-
ducting" angels, abundantly attested throughout the ample
literature of the Fathers,[9] for Christian antiquity was very
conscious of it. The reason is that the passage through
death is dangerous to souls and at this decisive moment
the devil still lies in wait for his prey. We need not be
surprised that the Church's prayer insists on this point.
Thus in the prayer *Commendo te*:

> May the foul Satan with all his evil spirits be forced to
> give way before thee; may he tremble at thy coming in
> the company of angels and flee away confounded into the
> vast chaos of eternal night. . . . May all the legions of hell

[9] On the rôle of St Michael in particular, cf. A. Baumstark,
Comparative Liturgy (London, 1958), p. 137.

be confounded and put to shame, and may none of the
ministers of Satan dare to stop thee in thy way . . .

It is in the same stream of exorcism that we should
place the very venerable prayer *Suscipe, Domine*:

> Deliver, O Lord, the soul of thy servant, as thou didst
> deliver [Adam from hell],[10]. . . Enoch and Elias from the
> common death of mankind; . . . Noah from the flood; . . .
> Abraham from Ur of the Chaldeans; . . . Job from his
> sufferings; . . . Isaac from being sacrificed at the hands of
> his father; . . . Lot from Sodom and the flame of fire; . . .
> Moses from the hand of Pharao, king of the Egyptians; . . .
> [the people of Israel from the depths of the sea; . . . Jonas
> from the belly of the whale;] . . . Daniel from the den of
> lions; . . . the three children from the furnace of burning
> fire; . . . Susanna from a false accusation; . . . David from
> the hand of King Saul and from the hand of Goliath; . . .
> Peter and Paul out of prison; . . . thy blessed Virgin Martyr
> Thecla from three most cruel torments.

This prayer, perhaps the oldest formula in the whole
ritual of a departing soul, certainly older than the fifth
century (since it is represented in the funerary art of the
earliest centuries and is itself undoubtedly inspired by a
Jewish prayer), appeals, by means of a number of Biblical
episodes, to the whole history of salvation and emphasizes
its quality of deliverance.

"Go forth, Christian soul." The Church has so gained
the mastery over death that for each of her sons she makes
it a sublime act of obedience and so of free self-offering.
To take over charge from her she has called on all the
angels and the saints, so that in his crossing from this
world to the next the Christian may not be left to face the

---

[10] The words between brackets do not appear in the Roman
Ritual but are taken from the Pontifical of Salzburg (*Ordo* of
Unction, Dom Martène's XII).

enemy powers alone. It remains only to entrust this soul
to God for eternity, as Christ himself entrusted his own
soul to his Father (Luke 23. 46):

> We commend to thee, O Lord, the soul of thy servant N.,
> and we pray thee, O Lord Jesus Christ, Saviour of the
> world, that as in mercy to him thou becamest man, so now
> thou wouldst vouchsafe to admit him to the bosom of thy
> patriarchs. Remember, O Lord, that he is thy creature, not
> made by strange gods, but by thee, the only living and true
> God ... May his soul rejoice, O Lord, in thy presence ...

Such is the last service rendered by the Church to the
one who has but a moment to live; a service often repeated
(in the prayers *Commendo te, Commendamus tibi, Tibi,
Domine, commendamus*), which has certainly given to the
entire ritual of departure its name of "Commendation of
the Soul":[11] not, of course, a "recommendation" in the
ordinary sense, but a handing over of powers, a transfer of
jurisdiction, after which the Church can act only *per
modum suffragii*, by intercession. In a sublime gesture the
Church returns the soul to God.

Such, then, in a deliberately logical order, are the prayers
for the dying. An inspection of the funeral rites will easily
reveal that the two groups have a mutual continuity of
inspiration. Here we can only recall the link between this
collection and the sacrament of the Viaticum, and by so
doing distinguish the character of initiation which marks
the Christian's death. Formerly, indeed, the Viaticum was
inserted directly in the ritual of departure, as in its authentic context.

It is not surprising, then, that the parallelism between

[11] We are aware that certain rituals use the term in another sense,
that is, the "committal" to the earth of the body of the departed,
but this use does not antedate the former.

entry into the Church and entry into eternal life is marked by some new traits: the fight against the devil, the escort of angels, the entry into the new Jerusalem are found in each. So, too, are the story of salvation (the prayer *Suscipe, Domine*) and the invocation of the Trinity (the prayers *Proficiscere, Commendamus tibi*: cf. the *Non intres in judicium* at burials). The lighted torches mentioned in the Commendation (in place of the candle which was once held by the dying man, though the rite is not retained in our present *ordo*),[12] remind us of the neophyte's candle and his sacramental "illumination". The welcome by the waiting saints corresponds to his welcome by the Christian community, when he came into the church from the baptistery. The psalms he sings or hears sung around him (*Confitemini Domino, Beati immaculati*; cf. *In exitu Israel* and *Quemadmodum desiderat cervus* of the ancient rituals) have a robustly Paschal character, and the same is true of the typology employed, the Red Sea, the Promised Land and the heavenly banquet.

The whole liturgy of death, centred on the Eucharist, sounds an absolutely triumphal note, where joy is entirely in place: *Haec dies quam fecit Dominus, exsultemus et laetemur in ea* (Psalm 117. 24). It is the great Christian paradox, founded on the victory of Christ, "who by his death has destroyed death and by his resurrection has restored life".[13] Thanks be to him, through whom our death will be both the perfect completion of our Christian initiation and the finished achievement of what was only its mystical anticipation, our "birth to heaven"!

---

[12] Certain customs are still in use, at least locally, such as lighting the Candlemas candle by the bed of the dying, but the meaning is not so much baptismal illumination as protection against the devil.

[13] Preface for Easter.

CONCLUSION

Suffering is an evil. Death is an evil. Both are the wages of sin (Rom. 6. 23). But Christ has conquered evil, on the one hand by mastering it through his miracles, on the other by taking it up into his redeeming Passion. Henceforth suffering and death have been transfigured for us, by the sacraments, which carry us into the depths of the Christian mystery.

Nothing is so beautiful, so overwhelming as this mystical transposition of the harshest facts of human life, through which faith pierces to uncover a new meaning, the meaning of the love, the life and the joy of paradise.

In these circumstances, why is our liturgy of the sick and dying so little understood by many Christians that we often hesitate to suggest—and to receive—Unction or the Viaticum? Only the history of Christian life through the ages could give the adequate and very complex answer to this question. But whatever the reasons for it, the supreme necessity is to remedy this state of affairs, and it is the Christian's training that is the point at issue.

Our Christians, by and large, are neither better nor worse than those of the past. Divine Truth, may we add, has not lost its power over souls. The whole secret of a renewal of Christian fervour lies, then, in the integral presentation of the Christian mystery. "Him I would learn to know, and the virtue of his resurrection, and what it means to share his sufferings, moulded into the pattern of his death, in the hope of achieving resurrection from the dead" (Philippians 3. 11).

We need not so much a morality as a *mystique*, or rather, a faith, to enable us to enter whole-heartedly into the Paschal mystery and to live by its principles for life and for death. Then surely we should understand that we can still be happy in the midst of life's trials and, above all, can welcome death as the Lord's summons to share in his own joy: "Well done, my good and faithful servant, come and share the joy of thy Lord" (Matt. 25. 21).

Such a faith is not purely notional, it is life-in-the-Spirit, in union with the whole Church, it is understanding of the Scriptures as read and interpreted by the Church, and active participation in her liturgy. It is by recovering the true dimensions of the sacred signs—we have seen how wide they are—that we shall enter personally into the sacred history of Salvation and that our life and our death, themselves become liturgy, will be identified with the glorious Easter of the Lord.

SELECT BIBLIOGRAPHY

(An asterisk denotes works by non-Catholics)

In this series: BECQUÉ, Maurice, C.SS.R., and BECQUÉ, Louis, C.SS.R.: *Life after Death.*

BOUYER, Louis, Cong. Orat.: *The Paschal Mystery*, London, Allen and Unwin, 1951; *Liturgical Piety* (English edn *Life and Liturgy*), Notre Dame, Ind., Notre Dame Univ. Press, 1955, and London, Sheed and Ward, 1956; *Christian Initiation*, London, Burns Oates, and New York, Macmillan, 1960.

ELLARD, Gerald, S.J.: *Christian Life and Worship*, revised edn, Milwaukee, Bruce, 1953.

*FROST, Evelyn: *Christian Healing*, London, Mowbray, 1949, and New York, Morehouse, 1950.

GASPARRI, Cardinal P.: *The Catholic Catechism*, London, Sheed and Ward, and New York, Kenedy, 1932.

GUARDINI, Romano: *The Last Things*, London, Burns Oates, and New York, Pantheon, 1954.

HOWELL, Clifford, S.J.: *Of Sacraments and Sacrifice* (English edn *The Work of our Redemption*), Collegeville, Minn, Liturgical Press, 1952, and Oxford, Catholic Social Guild, 1953.

JUNGMANN, J. A., S.J.: *Liturgical Worship* (English edn, *Public Worship*), New York, Pustet, 1941, and London, Challoner, 1957.

LEEMING, Bernard, S.J.: *Principles of Sacramental Theology*, London, Longmans, 1955, and Westminster, Md, Newman Press, 1956.

PALMER, Paul F., S.J.: *Sources of Christian Theology*: II, *Sacraments and Forgiveness*, London, Darton, Longman and Todd, 1960, and Westminster, Md, Newman Press, 1959.

PHILIPON, M. M., O.P.: *The Sacraments in the Christian Life*, London, Sands, 1954, and Westminster, Md, Newman Press, 1953.

*PULLER, F. W.: *The Anointing of the Sick in Scripture and Tradition*, London, S.P.C.K., 1904.

ROGUET, A. M., O.P.: *The Sacraments, Signs of Life*, London, Blackfriars, 1954.

The Small Ritual (Latin-English), London, Burns Oates, 1956.

WELLER, P.: *The Roman Ritual*, three volumes, Milwaukee, Bruce, 1946–52.

The Twentieth Century Encyclopedia of Catholicism

The number of each volume indicates its place in the over-all series and not the order of publication.

PART ONE: KNOWLEDGE AND FAITH

PART TWO: THE BASIC TRUTHS

All titles are subject to change.